The Road to Power

BY

KARL KAUTSKY

AUTHOR OF

"The Social Revolution," "Erfurter Program," "Origin of
Christianity," "Ethics and Materialistic Conception
of History," Etc., Etc.

AUTHORIZED TRANSLATION BY
A. M. SIMONS

1909
SAMUEL A. BLOCH
THE BOOKMAN
CHICAGO, ILL.

CONTENTS

CHAPTER I.

THE CONQUEST OF POLITICAL POWER.

Friends and enemies of the Socialists agree upon one thing, and that is that they constitute a REVOLUTIONARY party. But unfortunately the idea of revolution is many-sided, and consequently the conceptions of the revolution-ary character of our party differ very greatly. Not a few of our opponents insist upon understanding revolution to mean nothing else but anarchy, bloodshed, murder and arson. On the other hand there are some of our comrades to whom the coming social revolution appears to be noth-ing more than an extremely gradual, scarcely perceptible, even though ultimately a fundamental change in social relations, much of the same character as that produced by the steam engine.

So much is certain: that the Socialists, as the champions of the class interests of the proletariat, constitute a revolutionary party, because it is impos-sible to raise this class to a satisfactory existence within capitalist society; and because the liberation of the working class is only possible through the over-throw of private property in the means of production and rulership, and the substitution of social production for production for profit. The proletariat can attain to satisfaction of its wants only in a society whose institu-tions shall differ fundamentally from the present one. In still another way the Socialists are revolutionary. They recognize that the power of the state is an instru-ment of class domination, and indeed the most powerful instrument, and that the social revolution for which the proletariat strives cannot be realized until it shall have captured political power.

It is by means of these fundamental principles, laid down by Marx and Engels in the Communist Manifesto, that the Socialists of today are distinguished from the so-called Utopian Socialists of the first half of the last century, such as Owen and Fourier. It also distinguishes them from those who, like Proudhon, either treat the political struggle as unimportant, or else reject it entirely, and who believe it possible to bring about the economic transformation demanded by the interest of the proletariat through purely economic means without changing or capturing the power of the state.

In their recognition of the necessity of capturing political power Marx and Engels agreed with Blanqui. But while Blanqui thought it possible to capture the power of the state by a sudden act of a conspiratory minority, and then to use that power in the interest of the proletariat, Marx and Engels recognized that revolutions are not made at will. They come with inevitable necessity, when the conditions which render them necessary exist, and are impossible so long as those conditions, which develop gradually, do not exist. Only where the capitalist methods of production are highly developed is there the possibility of using the power of the state to transform capitalistic property in the means of production into social property. On the other hand, the possibility of capturing and holding the state for the proletariat only exists where the working class has grown to great proportions, is in large part firmly organized, and conscious of its class interests and its relation to state and society.

These conditions are being constantly created by the development of the capitalist methods of production and the class struggle between capitalists and laborers growing therefrom. So it is that just as the continuous expansion of capitalism necessarily and inevitably goes on, so the inevitable antithesis to this expansion, the proletarian revolution, proceeds equally inevitably and irresistibly.

It is irresistible, because it is inevitable that the growing proletariat should resist exploitation, and that it should organize industrially, co-operatively and politically to secure for itself better conditions of life and labor, and greater political influence. Everywhere the proletariat develops these phases of activity whether it is socialistically minded or not. It is the mission of the Socialist movement to bring all these various activities of the proletariat against its exploitation into one conscious and unified movement, that will find its climax in the great final battle for the conquest of political power.

This position, the fundamental principles of which were laid down in the Communist Manifesto, is today accepted by the Socialist movements of all countries. Upon it rests the whole great international Socialist movement of our time.

Meanwhile it is unable to proceed on its victorious way without finding doubters and critics within its own ranks.

To be sure, actual evolution has taken the road foretold by Marx and Engels. And the triumphant progress of Socialism is due, next to the extension of capitalism and therewith of the proletarian class struggle, above all to the keen analysis of the conditions and problems of this struggle supplied by the work of Marx and Engels.

In ONE point they were in error. THEY EXPECTED THE REVOLUTION TOO SOON.

The Communist Manifesto said at the end of 1847:

"The Communists turn their attention chiefly to Germany, because that country is on the eve of a bourgeois revolution, that is bound to be carried out under more advanced conditions of European civilization, and with a more developed proletariat than that of England was in the seventeenth, and of France in the eighteenth century, and because the bourgeois revolution in Germany will be but the prelude to an immediately following proletarian revolution."

The Manifesto was right in expecting a German revolution. But it was deceived when it believed this to be the immediate prelude to a proletarian revolution.

Nearer to us in time lies another prophecy made by Engels in an introduction to these conditions of Marx's brochure on the trial of the Cologne Communists, published in 1885. In this he stated that the next European uprising "was almost due, since the period of European revolutions during the present century was between 15 and 18 years—1815, 1830, 1848-52, 1870."

This expectation was not fulfilled, and up to the present time the expected revolution has not arrived.

Why was this? Was the Marxian method, upon which this expectation was based, false? In no way. But there was one factor in the calculation that was valued altogether too highly. Ten years ago I said concerning these very prophecies: "Both times the revolutionary and oppositional power of the capitalist class was overestimated."—(Neue Zeit, XVII: 2, p. 45.)

Marx and Engels expected a far-reaching and violent revolution in Germany in 1847 similar to the great French upheaval that began in 1789. Instead of this, however, there was but a wavering uprising that served only to frighten the whole capitalist class so that it took refuge under the wing of the government. The result was that the government was greatly strengthened and the rapid development of the proletariat was stifled. The bourgeoisie then relinquished to individual governments such further revolutionary action as was necessary to its progress. Bismarck, especially, was the great revolutionist of Germany, at least to the extent of throwing a few German princes from their thrones, favoring the unity of Italy, the dethroning of the Pope, and bringing about the overthrow of the empire and the introduction of the Republic in France.

This was the way in which the German bourgeois revolution, the early entrance of which Marx and Engels had prophesied in 1847, proceeded until it reached its end in 1870.

In spite of this Engels still expected a "political upheaval" in 1885, and declared that the "middle class democracy is even now the only party" that in case of such an uprising "must certainly come into power in Germany."

Again Engels prophesied truly in foretelling a "political upheaval," but again he was mistaken in expecting anything from the middle class democracy. This class failed completely when the Bismarckian regime collapsed. Consequently the overthrow of the Chancellor became only an act of the emperor, with no revolutionary consequences.

More and more it becomes evident that the only possible revolution is a *proletarian* revolution. Such a revolution is impossible so long as the organized proletariat does not form a body large enough and compact enough to carry, under favorable circumstances, the mass of the nation with it. But when once the proletariat comes to be the only revolutionary class in the nation, it necessarily follows that any crisis in an existing government, whether of a moral, financial or military nature, must include the bankruptcy of all capitalist parties, which as a whole are responsible, and in such a case the only government that could meet the situation would be a *proletarian* one.

Not all Socialists, however, draw these conclusions. There are some who, when an expected revolution does not come at the time set, do not draw the conclusion that industrial development may have altered the form and character of the coming revolution from what might have been expected from the experience of previous capitalist revolutions. On the contrary, they at once conclude that, under the changed conditions, revolutions are not to be expected, are not necessary, and indeed are hurtful.

On one side they conclude that a further extension of the achievements already gained—labor legislation, trade unions, co-operation—will suffice to drive the capitalist class out of one position after another, and to quietly expropriate it, without a political revolution, or any change in the nature of governmental power. This theory of the gradual growth into *(hineinwachsen)* the future state is a modern form of the old anti-political utopianism and Proudhonism.

On the other hand it is thought to be possible for the proletariat to obtain political power without a revolution, that is without any important transfer of power in the state, simply by a clever policy of co-operation with those bourgeois parties which stand nearest to the proletariat, and by forming a coalition government which is impossible for either party alone.

In this manner they think to get around a revolution as an outgrown barbaric method, which has no place in our enlightened century of democracy, ethics and brotherly love.

When this attitude is carried to its logical conclusion it throws the whole system of Socialist tactics founded by Marx and Engels into the street. The two cannot be reconciled. To be sure that is no reason why such a position should be declared false without examination. But it is a reason why everyone who, after careful study has become convicted of its erroneous character, should energetically oppose it, and this not merely because of a

difference of opinion, but because it means weal or woe
to the struggling workers.

It is very easy to be led into false paths in discussing
this question unless the boundaries of the subject are
narrowly defined.

Therefore it is necessary to make clear, what has so
often been stated before, that we are not discussing the
question of whether labor legislation and similar laws in
the interest of the proletariat, and unions and co-operatives are necessary and useful or not. There are no two
opinions among us on that point. What is disputed is
the view that the exploited class, who control the power
of the state, will permit such a development of these
factors, as will amount to abolishing capitalist oppression,
without first making such a resistance, with all the means
at its disposal, that it can be abolished only through a
decisive battle.

Furthermore this has nothing to do with the question
of utilizing quarrels among capitalist parties in the interest of the proletariat. It was not for nothing that Marx
and Engels fought the use of the phrase "reactionary
mass," because it tended to conceal the antagonism that
exists between different factions of the ruling class,
which may well be very important in securing the progress
of the working class. Laws for the protection of labor
and the extension of the suffrage are largely due to such
differences.

What is opposed is the idea of the possibility that a
proletarian party can during normal times regularly combine with a capitalist party for the purpose of maintaining a *government* or a *governmental party*, without being
destroyed by the insuperable conflicts which must exist.
The power of the state is everywhere an organ of class
rule. The class antagonisms between the workers and
the possessing class are so great that the proletariat can
never share governmental power with any possessing

class. The possessing class will always demand, and its
interests will force it to demand, that the power of the
state shall be used to hold the proletariat down. On the
other hand the proletariat will always demand that any
government in which their own party possesses power,
shall use the power of the state to assist it in its battle
against capital. Consequently every government based
upon a coalition of capitalist and working class parties is
foredoomed to disruption.

A proletarian party which shares power with a capitalist party in any government must share the blame for any
acts of subjection of the working class. It thereby invites
the hostility of its own supporters, and this in turn causes
its capitalist allies to lose confidence and makes any progressive action impossible. No such arrangement can
bring any strength to the working class. No capitalist
party will permit it do so. It can only compromise a
proletarian party and confuse and split the working class.

It was just such a condition that constantly postponed
the revolution of 1848 and brought about the political
collapse of the bourgeois democracy, and excluded any
co-operation with it for the purpose of winning and utilizing political power.

However willing Marx and Engels were to utilize the
differences between capitalist parties for the furtherance
of proletarian purposes, and however much they were
opposed to the expression "reactionary mass," they have,
nevertheless, coined the phrase *"dictation of the proletariat,"* which Engels defended shortly before his death in
·1891, as expressing the fact that only through purely
proletarian political domination can the working class
exercise its political power.

Even if an alliance between capitalist and working-class
political parties is incapable of contributing to the development of proletarian power, and even if the progress of
social reform and economic organization must be limited

under the present conditions, and even if because of these facts the political revolution has NOT YET come, this does not give the slightest reason for concluding that therefore revolutions belong to the past and there never will be any in the future.

Others who doubt the coming of a revolution are not so dogmatic in their conclusions. They recognize that revolutions may still come, but say that if one comes it will be in the far distant future. For at least a generation it is wholly impossible. So far as practical politics are concerned it is not to be taken into our calculations. For the next decade at least we must depend upon the policy of peaceful permeation and the alliance with capitalist parties.

Yet facts are just now arising that more than ever before tend to show the weakness of this view.

CHAPTER II.

PROPHECIES OF THE REVOLUTION.

In order to discredit the expectations of a revolution by the Marxians, we are frequently reproached with the statement that while we dearly love to prophesy, we are very poor prophets.

We have already seen why it was that the proletarian revolution expected by Marx and Engels has not yet appeared. When, however, we turn from this one disappointed expectation, astonishment arises, not that all their prophecies have not been realized, but that they were able accurately to foretell so much.

For example, we have already called attention to the fact that in November, 1847, the Communist Manifesto had already announced the revolution of 1848. This was at the very time when Proudhon was proving that the era of revolutions had gone forever.

Marx was the first Socialist to point out the significance of the trade unions in the proletarian class struggle. He did this in his controversial work against Proudhon, "The Misery of Philosophy," in 1846. His work upon "Capital" shows that during the '70's he already foresaw the growth of the corporations and the trusts of today. During the war of 1870-71 he prophesied that henceforth the center of gravity of the Socialist movement would pass from France to Germany. In January, 1873, he prophesied the crisis that had its beginning a few months later, etc.

The same is true of Engels.

Even when they were mistaken there was always a very accurate and important kernel of truth in the midst of the error. Remember, for example, what has just been said about the expectations that Engels expressed in 1885 concerning the political upheavals of the next few years.

Here is a good place to refute a legend that has of late gained considerable credence. In his work on "The Labor Question," a fifth edition of which has just appeared, Professor H. Herkner of Berlin writes as follows concerning the report of the Socialist Congress at Hanover in 1899:

"In the heat of the debate Kautsky was led to designate the hope of an early catastrophe that would fulfill all wishes, as idiocy and to attack this idea far sharper than even Bernstein had done. If Engels actually had predicted the coming of a great catastrophic collapse (Klatterdatsch) in 1898 (said Kautsky) then he would not have been the great thinker that he was, but such an idiot that not a single district would have chosen him as a delegate to the convention. Engels meant nothing more than to say that by 1898 the present Prussian political system might collapse.

"There may be some uncertainty as to what Engels meant. On the other hand the statement of Bebel's at the Erfurter Convention in 1891, that there were but few members of that body but would live to see the realization of the final goal, admits of no saving explanation. This statement was, to use Kautsky's expression, idiotic. This is the way in which the confusion that reigns in the heads of the defenders of the old tactics is gradually gaining as clear and satisfactory expression as could be wished."—p. 379.)

. Unfortunately the professor's clearness leaves much to
· be desired. I have never designated as idiotic "the hope
of an early catastrophe that would fulfill all wishes (!)"
for the simple reason that no one was talking about any
such thing. I would certainly be justified in calling the
hope of an *"all-wishes-fulfilling"* catastrophe idiotic. I
applied the word "idiocy" to the statement that Engels
had ever set a DEFINITE DATE for the outbreak of the
revolution in 1898. Any prophecy of this sort would
certainly seem to me to be idiotic. But Engels was never
guilty of anything of the kind. Just as little was Bebel.
Nor did he, at the Erfurter Convention, set any definite
date for the coming of the revolution.

There were some who made fun of his "prophesying"
at that time. To these he made this reply:

"You may laugh and sneer at prophesying, but
thinking men can not avoid it. There was a time,
not so many years ago, when even Vollmar did not
assume this attitude of cold pessimistic darkness.
Engels, whom he has been attacking, correctly foretold the revolution of 1848 in 1844. And furthermore was not everything prophesied by Marx and
Engels in the well known address of the International Workingmen's Association at the time of the
Commune uprising, concerning the future of events
in Europe, fulfilled even to the dotting of an i.
(That's right.) Liebknecht, who has been making a
little fun of me on this point, has done his share of
prophesying. (Laughter.) Like me, he prophesied
certain things in the Reichstag in 1870 which have
since been completely fulfilled. Read his speeches
and mine from 1870-1871 and you will find the proof
of this. But now comes Vollmar and cries: 'Keep
still about your ancient history and stop prophesying.' But he also has done some prophesying. The

only difference between him and me is that he has the most wonderful optimism in regard to our opponents, and the most fearful pessimism in regard to the principal aims of the party and its future."—(Proceedings of Congress, p. 283.)

One of the most significant of the prophecies of Bebel which has been fulfilled was the one which he made in 1873 that the Center, which then had sixty seats, would soon have a hundred, and that the Bismarckian fight on the Catholic Center (Kulturkampf) would have a miserable end, and would contribute to Bismarck's overthrow.

Recently some have done me the honor to place me in the ranks of the "prophets." I could not well be in better company.

I have been reproached with some of the things that I wrote in the series of articles in the Neue Zeit and in the introduction to my work on Ethics concerning the revolution, which it is claimed the course of events proved fundamentally wrong.

Is this correct?

In the introduction to my "Ethics" I wrote:

"We are about to enter upon a period, whose length no one knows, during which no Socialist can engage in quiet labors, but where our work must be that of constant fighting. * * * The tools of the Czar are eager in their work as were the Albas and the Tillys in the religious wars of the sixteenth and seventeenth centuries—not with deeds of military heroism, but of brutal murder and arson. The West European champions of law and order defend these actions as restoring legal conditions. But just as little as the soldiers of the Hapsburgs, in spite of momentary successes, were able to restore Catholicism in North Germany and Holland, are the Cossacks of the Romanoffs capable of restoring the regime of absolutism. The Czar has the power to lay his country waste, but he never more can govern it.

"In any case the Russian revolution is far from being at an end. It cannot end so long as the Russian peasants are not satisfied. The longer it continues the greater will be the unrest of the masses of the workers of Western Europe, the nearer the danger of financial catastrophes, and the more probable that an era of acute class struggles will begin in Western Europe."

What is there in these words, written in January, 1906, of which I should now be ashamed? Does anyone believe that the Russian revolution is at an end and that normal conditions are now prevailing in Russia? And is it not true that since the above lines were written the whole world has been in a condition of great unrest?

And now about my "unfortunate prophecy" in my "Various Phases of Revolution." I was there writing a polemic against Lusnia, who declared it impossible that a war over Corea could lead to a Revolution in Russia, and claimed that I exaggerated when I pronounced the Russian laborers a much more vital political factor than the English. On these points I replied as follows in February, 1904, at the beginning of the Russo-Japanese war:

"There is no doubt that the economic development of Russia is far behind that of Germany or England, and that its proletariat is much weaker and less mature than the German or the English. But all things are relative, including the revolutionary power of a class."

I explained the reasons that made the Russian proletariat such an extraordinary revolutionary force, and continued:

"The more completely Western Europe withholds its help from absolutism, the quicker will it be over-thrown. To assist to this end, to discredit Czarism as much as possible, is today the most important work of the International Socialist movement. * * *

"Meanwhile, in spite of all his valuable friendships in Western Europe, the Autocrat of the Russias grows visibly less powerful. The war with Japan may greatly hasten the progress of the Russian revo-lution. * * * What took place after the Russo-Turkish war will be repeated in a higher degree: a great extension of the revolutionary movement." Having established this point, I continued:

"A revolution in Russia cannot at once establish a Socialist regime. The economic conditions of the country are not sufficiently developed for that. The best it can do is to bring a democratic government into existence, behind which would be a strong and impetuous and progressive proletariat that would be able to demand important concessions.

"Such a regime in Russia could not but have pow-erful counter effects upon neighboring countries. First by reviving and inspiring the proletarian move-ment itself, giving it thereby the impulse to attack the political obstacles to an actual democracy—in Prussia, primarily the "three-class" electoral system. Secondly, through the release of the manifold na-tional questions of Western Europe."

I wrote this in February, 1904. In October, 1905, the Russian Revolution was a reality and the proletariat was its champion, while at the same time its reactions were being felt upon neighboring lands. In Austria the battle for universal suffrage gained irresistible force and pressed on to victory. Hungary was on the verge of actual in-surrection. The German Socialists accepted the principle of the general strike, and threw its full force into the fight for suffrage, especially in Prussia, where it led to actual street demonstrations, in January, 1908, something that had not been seen in Berlin since 1848. And in 1907 came the hysterical elections and the complete collapse of the German democracy. When I had expressed an expectation of the release of the nationalistic movements of Eastern Europe, these expectations were far exceeded by the rapid awakening of the entire Orient—in China, India, Egypt, Morocco, Persia and Turkey. In the last two countries especially this awakening has culminated in successful revolutionary uprisings.

And in connection with this we have had a steady sharpening of national antagonisms that have twice already, first in Morocco and then in Turkey, led Europe to the verge of war.

If ever there was a "prophecy," if you wish to use the word, that has been completely fulfilled, it was this one of the coming of the Russian revolution and that it would bring with it an era of increased political unrest and a sharpening of all social and national antagonisms.

Certainly I will not deny that I did not foretell the momentary defeat of the Russian revolution. But did the person who in 1846 foretold the revolution of 1848 make a mistake because it was put down in 1849?

Certainly we must recognize the possibility of defeat in the case of every great movement or uprising. Only the fool sees victory already in his pocket before he enters upon a battle. All we can do is to investigate and decide whether we shall enter upon a great revolutionary struggle. We can determine this question with certainty. But the outcome of such a struggle cannot be foretold. We would be a miserable sort of fellows, and, indeed, direct traitors to our cause, and incapable of any fight, if we overlooked the possibility of defeat and reckoned only upon victory.

Naturally every expectation cannot be fulfilled. Anyone who pretends to be an infallible prophet, or who demands infallible prophecies of others, presupposes supernatural powers in men.

Every student of politics must calculate upon the possibility of the defeat of his expectations. From this it does not necessarily follow that "prophesying" is foolish play, but, on the contrary, when carefully and methodically done, it is a part of the continuous work of every thinking and far-seeing political worker, as Bebel has already proven.

Only the most brainless routine worker is satisfied with the belief that things will continue to be as they now are. The politician, who is also a thinker, will weigh every possibility that each coming event may carry in itself, and think them out to their furtherest consequences. To be sure, the power of inertia in society is enormous. In nine cases out of ten the follower of precedent will be right when he follows the old road, without worrying about new situations and possibilities. But on the one time there will come an event strong enough to overcome this power of inertia, that has perhaps already been internally weakened by previous conditions, while externally everything remained the same. Then suddenly evolution starts out upon new roads. The followers of routine lose their heads. Only those politicians are able to assert themselves who have been considering new possibilities and their consequences.

It does not even follow that even in the customary run of events the brainless follower of routine is superior to the "prophesying" politician who weighs the future. This can be true only when the politician treated the possibilities whose consequences he had calculated, as realities, and directed his practical acts accordingly. Will anyone claim that Engels and Bebel and other similar "prophesying" politicians that we have been discussing have ever understood their prophecies in this sense?

The brainless follower of routine will never feel himself compelled to study present conditions, which to him are simple repetitions of already well-known situations, in which he has already been moving. Whoever, on the contrary, considers all the possibilities and consequences of a given situation must carefully study all the forces and powers that it presents. In so doing his attention would naturally be turned first of all to the most recently developed and least considered factors.

What many a Philistine looks upon as a purposeless building of castles in the air, is in reality the result of the deepest study, and consequently is based upon the most careful consideration of reality. Bebel and Engels can be criticised for their "prophecies," only if these can be shown to be impractible phantasies. As a matter of fact, no one has shown a greater ability in advising the proletariat in times of desperate need, or has given more valuable guidance, than just these "prophets." This was just because they were occupied with the work of "prophesying." It has not been the politicians with the widest visions who have most frequently misled the rising class, but rather those "practical politicians" who could not see further than their noses, and who considered only those things to be real which they could touch with their noses, and who pronounced every obstacle endless and unconquerable against which they bloodied their noses.

But there is still another form of "prophecy" besides that described above. In the last analysis the development of any society is determined by the development of its method of production. We are today sufficiently familiar with these laws to recognize the direction which social evolution must take, and to determine the road the political happenings must take.

This sort of "prophesying" is frequently confused with

what we have been discussing, and yet the two are fundamentally different. In the one case we are dealing with
a great mass of possibilities which may be contained in
any particular situation or event, and whose possible consequences we must determine. In the other case we are
dealing with a single necessary line of evolution, knowledge of which we are seeking. In the first case we are
concerned with definite, concrete facts. In the other
we can only point out general tendencies, without being
able to say anything definite regarding the form they will
take. These two forms of investigation must not be confused, even though they appear to give the same result.

When, for example, one person says that a war between
France and Germany would lead to a revolution, and
when another declares that the constantly increasing class
antagonisms in capitalist society will lead to a revolution,
it seems as if the latter prophecy of a revolution was of
the same nature as the first. Yet they are fundamentally
very different.

When I speak of a war between France and Germany
I am not talking of an event, the appearance of which
can be determined with the certainty of a law of nature.
Science has not yet reached that point. Such a war is
only one of very many possibilities. On the other hand,
a revolution which comes from such a war must be of
certain definite forms. It may happen that in the weaker
of the two warring countries the effort to unite all
the forces of the state against the external enemy may
bring the most daring and energetic class—the proletariat—to the head of the nation. This was what Engels
thought possible in 1891 in Germany when a war was
expected between Germany and the then relatively more
populous France, and when Russia was still unconquered
and not disrupted by revolution.

Revolution as a result of war can only come from an
uprising of the mass of the people. This would come

when the power of the army was broken and the nation was surfeited with the misery of war. The government would then be overthrown, not in order to prosecute the war more energetically, but to end a useless and accursed war with an opponent who also desired nothing more than the end.

Again, revolution as the result of war may arise as a result of a universal uprising against a disgraceful and especially injurious treaty of peace. Such an uprising might easily combine the army and the people.

In such cases the form of the revolution can be determined in advance. But it is impossible to form any picture of the revolution which I can foretell as a result of the increased sharpening of class antagonisms. I can state with certainty that a revolution brought on by war will take place during the war or immediately after it. On the other hand, when I speak of a revolution as the result of increased sharpening of class antagonisms, this tells us absolutely nothing as to the time it will appear.

I can say definitely that a revolution brought about by a war will happen but once. Nothing whatever can be said on this point concerning the revolution springing from sharpening class antagonisms. It may be a long-drawn-out process, while a revolution as the result of war must take on more the character of a single event. It is impossible to say in advance whether a revolution as the result of war would be successful. The revolutionary movement springing out of class antagonisms, on the contrary, cannot meet with anything more than temporary defeats, and must ultimately win.

On the other hand, the preliminary conditions to a revolution in the first case—that of war—are something which may or may not appear. No one can possibly say anything definite on this point. The sharpening of class antagonism, on the contrary, arises inevitably out of the laws of the capitalist method of production. While a revolution as the result of war is only one of many possibilities, as the result of class antagonisms, it is inevitable.

It is evident that each sort of "prophecy" demands its own especial method, and its own especial study, and that the significance of the "prophecy" depends upon the thoroughness of such study, instead of being, as some people who have no conception of the amount of such studying seem to think, mere empty phantasies.

It would be very much of a mistake, however, to conclude that we Marxians are the only ones that prophesy. Even bourgeois politicians, who are standing on the basis of the present state of affairs, are not without their visions of a distant future. The whole force of colonial politics, for example, rests on this fact. If we were dealing with colonial policy for today only it would be easy to do away with it. For every country but England it is a miserable business. But it is the only field inside capitalist society from which great hopes for the future at least appear to beckon. And therefore, because of the glittering future which our colonial fanatics prophesy, and not because of the miserable present, colonial politics exercise such a fascinating attraction to such minds as are not convinced of the coming of Socialism.

Nothing is more foolish than the idea that distant ideals have no practical significance in present politics that immediate interests always rule, or that we will be successful in our electoral agitation in proportion as we are "practical"—which signifies insipid and insignificant, and the more we talk only of taxes and tariffs, police graft and sick insurance and similar things, and the more we treat our future goal as a youthful love affair, to be cherished in our hearts and looked back to with longing, but to which it is best not to make any reference in public.

CHAPTER III.

There is no such thing as politics without prophesying. The only difference is that those who prophesy that things will always remain the same do not know that they are prophesying.

Naturally there can be no proletarian politician who is satisfied with present conditions and does not strive fundamentally to alter them. And there is no intelligent politician, of whatever faction, who possesses even a remnant of freedom of judgment who is not forced to recognize that political conditions cannot remain as they now are in the midst of the present rapid rate of economic transformation.

But if in spite of this he refuses to recognize the possibility of a political revolution, that is, of a decided rearrangement of political power in the state, then there is nothing left for him to do but to seek in some way gradually and imperceptibly to do away with class antagonism without any great decisive battle.

The reformers dream of the establishment of social peace between the classes, between exploited and exploiters, without abolishing exploitation. They would bring this about by having each class exercise a certain self-restraint toward the other, and by the giving up of all "excesses" and "extreme demands." There are people who believe that the antagonisms which exist between the individual laborer and capitalist would disappear if they

26

confronted each other in ORGANIZED form. Wage contracts are to be the beginning of social peace. In reality organization simply concentrates the antagonisms. The struggle becomes less frequent, but more violent, and disturbs society far more than former little individual conflicts. The antagonism of conflicting interests becomes much harsher. Because of the existence of organization the conflict tends to drop its character of a *momentary* conflict of *individual persons,* and takes on the form of a NECESSARY conflict between whole CLASSES.

It is impossible for a Socialist to share the illusion of the reconciliation of classes and the coming of social peace. That he does not share it is what makes him a Socialist. He knows that if social peace is to come it will be not by a chimerical RECONCILIATION, but by the ABOLITION of classes. When he has lost faith in a revolution, however, there is nothing left for him but to await the peaceful and imperceptible disappearance of classes through economic progress—through the growth and increased power of the working class, which gradually absorbs the other classes.

That is the theory of the gradual growth into *(hineinwachsen)* the socialist society.

This theory contains a germ of truth. It is supported by facts of economic development that show an actual growth toward Socialism. It was Marx and Engels who first set forth these facts and explained the scientific laws that govern them.

We are growing from two directions. One of these is through the development of capitalism, and the concentration of capital. When, in the competitive struggle a larger body of capital is brought into conflict with a smaller the latter is first pressed, then oppressed, and finally suppressed. This fact, wholly apart from the rage for profits, compels every capitalist to increase his capital and to extend his undertakings. Ever larger grow the industries, ever more and more industries are concentrated in a single hand. Today we have reached the point where banks and promoting organizations control and direct the greater part of the capitalist undertakings in the various countries. So it is that the road is being prepared for the social organization of production.

Hand in hand with this centralization of business goes the growth of great fortunes, something that is in no way hindered by the appearance of the corporation. On the contrary, the corporation not only makes the control of production by a few banks and industrial combines possible; it also furnishes a means by which the very smallest fortunes can be transformed into capital and thereby be made to contribute to the centralizing process on capitalism.

Through the corporation the savings of even the poor are placed at the disposal of the great capitalists, who are enabled to use those savings as if they were a part of their great capitals. As a result the centralizing power of their own great fortunes is increased still more.

The corporation renders the person of the capitalist wholly superfluous for the conduct of capitalist undertakings. The exclusion of his personality from industrial life ceases to be a question of POSSIBILITY or of INTENTION. It is purely a question of POWER.

This preparation for Socialism through the concentration of capital is meanwhile only one side of the process of gradual growth into the future state. Along with it there is proceeding an evolution within the working class that is no less of an indication of growth in the direction of Socialism.

With the growth of capital goes also an increase in the number of proletarians within society. They become the most numerous class. Simultaneously grows their organization. The laborers create co-operatives that abolish the middle men and establish production directly for their own use. They organize unions that restrict the absolute power of the employers and exercise an influence in the productive process. They elect members to the representative bodies in the municipalities and states who seek to secure reforms, to enact legislation for the protection of laborers, to make state and municipal industries model businesses and to increase the number of such industries.

These movements go on continuously, so that our reformers say we are in the midst of the social revolution, indeed some of them would say in the midst of Socialism. All that is needed is further development along these lines, with no catastrophe—indeed, anything of the kind would only disturb this gradual growth into Socialism. Therefore, away with all such ideas, let us concentrate on "positive" work.

This outlook is certainly a very alluring one, and a person would have to be a regular fiend to wish to destroy such a magnificent "gradual reformist ascension" by any sort of catastrophe. Were the wish father to our thought we Marxists would all become inspired with this idea of a gradual growth.

It has only one little defect: The growth that it describes is not the growth of a SINGLE element, but of TWO elements, and, moreover, of two very ANTAGONISTIC elements—Capital and Labor. What appears to the "reformers" as a peaceable growth into Socialism, is only the growth in power of two antagonistic classes, standing in irreconcilable enmity to each other. This phenomena means nothing more or less than that the antagonism between Capitalist and Laborer, which, in the beginning, existed only between a number of individuals, constituting together but a minority in the state, has now become a battle between gigantic, compact organizations that dominate and determine our whole social and political life,

So it is that this gradual growth into Socialism is really a gradual growth into great struggles that shatter the very base of the state, that is growing ever more violent, and that can end only with the overthrow and expropriation of the capitalist class. It must so end, because the working class is indispensable for society. It may be temporarily defeated, but it can never be destroyed. The capitalist class, on the contrary, has become superfluous. The first great defeat that it receives in the struggle for control of the state must lead to its complete and final collapse.

Those who do not recognize that this gradual growth into Socialism includes these consequences must be blind to the fundamental fact of our society—the class antagonisms between capitalists and laborers.

This growth into Socialism is only another expression for the steady sharpening of class antagonisms, for the growth into an epoch of greater, more decisive class struggles, such as we have described under the name of the Social Revolution.

To be sure, the revisionists do not grant this position. But up to the present time none of them has been able to bring any convincing argument against it. The exceptions that they offer, when of any importance, indicate, not a "growth into" Socialism, but a "growth away" from Socialism. Such is the case, for example, with the acceptance of the idea that Capital is not concentrating, but the reverse. This logical contradiction is bound up with the very essence of revisionism. It must accept the Marxian theory of capitalism in order to prove the growth toward Socialism. It must discard this theory in order to make credible the peaceable, progressive development of society and the softening of class antagonisms.

A glimmering of this idea is beginning to penetrate the heads of the revisionists and their neighbors, and they are beginning to see that the idea of a peaceable growth into the future state has a catch in it.

In this connection an article by Nauman, published in the October number of the "Neuen Rundshau" (1908) and later in the "Hilfe," on "The Fate of Marxism," is very significant. It is a pretty rough fate that the former leader of the National Social party pictures for us. He concludes that the concentration of capital and the formation of Employers' Associations have surprised us Marxians, and placed us in an unexpected dilemma. This good man has no suspicion of the fact that it was Marx who first set forth the existence of these very things upon the continent of Europe, and that he recognized their significance long before even other Socialists.

But we have become accustomed to ignorance of such things on the part of these gentlemen, and it does not require further attention here. It is worthy of notice, however, that Nauman, in his article, discovers the superiority of concentrated capital so that, according to him, economic evolution is not leading to Socialism, but to a "new feudalism, with inconceivably powerful economic means." Against the Employers' association, he says, co-operatives and unions cannot prevail.

"For any conceivable time the leadership of industry must be located where the trusts and the banks work together. There is growing up a rulership that cannot be thrown from the saddle by any social revolution, so long as there do not come times of unemployment that shall release the hunger rage of the masses, that will blindly throw everything overboard without being able to erect anything better in its place. The idea of a social revolution is practically at an end. All this is very painful for the old-style Socialists, and also for us social ideologists, who have been hoping for a swifter gait in the progress of

Labor. But it makes no difference how much we may have deceived ourselves—the future belongs to the industrial combinations."

That certainly does not look like growing into Socialism, and least of all like a peaceful growth. Nauman, himself, can suggest no other way of overthrowing this feudalism than a "popular rage" *(Massengroll)*, that shall "throw everything overboard"—that is a revolution, and he reaches this conclusion by a logical somersault. First he asserts that the employers' associations can be overthrown only by a revolution. Then he avoids the idea of this sort of a revolution by the simple assertion that it must be a hunger revolt, which "would simply throw everything overboard, without being able to erect anything better in its place." Why this must be so, why the revolution is doomed beforehand to barrenness remains Nauman's secret.

After having killed the idea of a revolution with a stroke of his pen, without any reason, he by no means sinks into complete hopelessness. On the contrary, he arises filled with joyous faith. He then discovers that the employers' associations are invincible only to Marxians who recognize economic necessity and deny free will. We have only to recognize this will and we can handle the employers' associations, and the "inconceivably great power" of the "new feudalism" loses its invincibleness.

What is not possible to the uprising of the masses can be accomplished by the recognition of the free will of the individual—of his "personality." The proof of this is furnished by "practical politics."

Nauman tells us:

"Marx cared little for appeals to free will, since he looked upon all events as determined by natural necessity. At least, it sounds that way in his theory.

As an individual man, to be sure, he was a personality with a powerful will, who aroused to energetic action. Today there is with the thinking portion of the Socialist movement a certain wandering back from this philosophy of nature to a philosophy of the will, and consequently to the fundamental philosophy of the Socialist movement. Edward Bernstein has spoken the plainest on this point, calling for a return to the feet of Kant. In the anarchist or half-anarchist movement that accompanies Socialism we find this same tendency away from the belief in a blindly ruled natural history in economic life, toward the view that the will can form things as it wishes. This return to the idea of the will is a result of the fact of the permanence of the new industrial domination. One is forced to recognize that it will not overthrow itself, but that concessions can be obtained from it through acts of the will."

The "ones" who have recognized this are just those worshipers of the gradual growth into Socialism. We Marxists do not really need this knowledge. For the revisionists, as well as their anarchist and National Social assistants, on the contrary, this is a wonderful discovery. But they are bees that know how to get honey out of every flower, and they are therefore able to see, even in this discovery, a complete overthrow of the Marxian position, and the same is true of their liberal, National Social, anarchist and half-anarchist intellectual brothers. They all complain that Marx recognized only a "blindly ruled," "automatic," economic evolution, and knew nothing of the human will. And it should be our main task to arouse this will.

So teaches, not alone Nauman, but also Friedeberg. So teaches all those elements within the Socialist movement that are vibrating between Nauman and Friedeberg, and so teach also the theoreticians of revisionism like Tuganbaranowsky:

"The author of 'Capital' overvalued the significance of the elementary side of the historical process, and did not comprehend the tremendous creative role of the living human personality in this process."—(Der Moderne Socialismus, p. 91.)

All this shows clearly that the theory of the "gradual growth into" Socialism has a large hole that is to be stopped up by the tremendous creative role of the living human personality and its free will. But this free will that is to bring about the "gradual growth" really means its abolition. If Nauman is right, and the will is free and can "shape things as it wishes," then it can also "shape as it wishes" the direction of economic development. Then it is absolutely impossible to discover any guarantee that we are growing into Socialism. It is, moreover, impossible to determine any line of historical development whatsoever, and no scientific knowledge of society is possible.

CHAPTER IV.

ECONOMIC EVOLUTION AND THE WILL.

The revisionists meet these conclusions with the claim that there is a much greater contradiction in Marx himself. They allege that, as a thinker, he recognized no such thing as a free will, but expected everything to come from inevitable economic evolution, which moves on automatically, but that as a revolutionary fighter he sought in the strongest manner to develop wills, and to appeal to the volition of the proletariat. This proves Marx to be guilty of an irreconcilable contradiction between theory and practice, declare the revisionists, anarchists and liberals in closest harmony.

In reality Marx is guilty of no such contradiction. It is a product of the confusion of his critics—a confusion that is incurable, since it recurs again and again. It rests in the first place in the making of will and free will identical. Marx has never failed to recognize the significance of the will and the "tremendous role of human personality" in society. He has only denied the freedom of the will, something very different. This has been explained so often that it scarcely seems necessary to restate it here.

Furthermore, this confusion rests upon a most remarkable conception of the meaning of economics and economic development. All these learned gentlemen seem to think that because this evolution proceeds according to certain definite laws it is automatic and spontaneous without the willing human personality. For them the human will is a separate element *alongside of* and *above* economics. It adds to the force and operates upon economics, "making otherwise" the things produced by economics. Such a view is only possible in minds that have only a scholastic conception of economics, that have gathered their ideas entirely from books, and that treat it purely intellectually, without the slightest vital conception of the actual economic process. Here, at least, the proletariat is superior to them, and in spite of Maurenbrecher and Eisner, is better capable of comprehending this process and its historic role, than the capitalist theoretician to whom economic practice is foreign, or than the capitalist practical man to whom every theoretical interest is foreign, and who has no conception of the necessity of understanding anything more of economics than is essential to successful profit making.

All economic theory becomes mere mental gymnastics for those who do not proceed from the knowledge that the motive force back of every economic event is the human will. Certainly not a FREE will, not a will existing by itself *(Wollen an sich)*, but a PREDETERMINED *(bestimmtes)* will. It is, in the last analysis, the WILL TO LIVE which lies at the basis of all economics, which appeared with life as soon as it was gifted with movement and sensation. Every expression of the will is, in the last analysis, to be traced back to the will to live.

Whatever especial forms this life impulse *(Lebenswille)* of an organism may take in individual cases depends upon the conditions of that life, taking the word condition in the widest possible sense, as including all the dangers and limitations of life, not merely the means of its sustenance. The conditions of life determine the character of its volition, the nature of its acts and their results.

This knowledge forms the starting point of the materialistic conception of history. But, to be sure, the simplicity of the relations, that must be explained in this manner in the less complex organisms, give place in higher organisms to conditions in which many intermediate members step in between the mere will to live and the manifold forms of its expression.

I cannot here undertake to carry this further. But a few suggestions may be given.

The conditions of life of an organism are of a twofold nature—first, those that are continually repeated and that do not change in the course of many generations. A will developed by and adjusted to such conditions is strengthened both by inherited custom and natural selection. It becomes an instinct, an impulse which the individual follows under all circumstances, even under extraordinary conditions where following it does not maintain and sustain life, but injures it, perhaps even leads to death. In spite of all this the basis of this will is still the will to live.

mysticism

Alongside of those conditions of life that are constantly repeated there are also others that appear only seldom or in changed form. Here instinct fails. Here the maintenance of life depends fundamentally upon the possession of intelligence by the organism which will enable it to recognize a given situation and to adjust itself to it. The more an animal form lives in swiftly changing conditions of life the more its intelligence is developed. This is partly due to the fact that the organ of intelligence has greater demands put upon it and partly because the individuals with weaker intelligence are more quickly eliminated.

Finally, when we come to man, intelligence has grown so great that he is able to construct artificial organs—weapons and tools—with which the better to assert himself under given conditions of life. But at the same time he creates for himself new conditions to which, in turn, he must adapt himself. So it is that technical development, a result of higher intelligence, becomes in turn an impulse to further development of intelligence.

Technical development is also a result of the will to live, but it carries with it important modifications of that will. The animal wishes to live just because it is alive. It demands nothing more. The discovery of new weapons or new tools brings with it the power of living better than before. It brings the possibility of more abundant nourishment, greater leisure, better security, and finally the satisfaction of new necessities than has hitherto been possible. The higher technical evolution, the more the will to LIVE becomes the will to live BETTER.

This will is the distinguishing mark of civilized man.

Technical evolution changes not only the relation of man to nature, but also that between man and man.

Man belongs to the social animals. The conditions for his life cannot be met in isolation, but demand the formation of societies. The will to live takes on the form of the will to live with and for the members of a society. Technical development changes, among other conditions of life, the forms of social life and co-operation. It does this primarily by bestowing organs upon man that are separated from his body. The natural tools and weapons, nails, teeth, horns and the like, are the property of all individuals of the same nature, and of the same age and sex. The artificial tools and weapons, on the other hand, may all be possessed by a single individual, who may withhold them from all others. Those who have the control of such tools and weapons live under different conditions of life from those who are deprived of them. So different classes are created, in each of which the same will to live takes a different form.

A capitalist, for example, according to the conditions under which he lives, cannot exist without profit. His will to live drives him to acquire profits, and his will to live better forces him to seek increased profits. This, again, compels him to increase his capital; in the same manner and to an even higher degree, the competitive struggle threatens him with destruction, if he is not able continuously to increase his capital. The concentration of capital is not an automatic process, that proceeds without the will and the consciousness of the participants. It would not be possible without the energetic will of the capitalists to become rich and to drive their weaker competitors out of the field. What does lie outside their will and their consciousness is the simple fact that the result of their willing and striving is to create the necessary · conditions for Socialist production. That the capitalists certainly do not wish. But this does not say that in the economic process, the volition of man, and the "gigantic role of creative personality" is excluded.

The same will to live that animates the capitalists, exists also among the workers. But it takes on different forms to correspond with the different conditions of life. It is not expressed in a struggle for profits, but for sale of labor power, for higher prices for labor power, and lower prices for the means of life; out of this springs the creation of unions and co-operatives, the seeking after legislation for the protection of labor, and finally out of this springs a second tendency, accompanying the concentration of capital, that may be designated as a growing into Socialism. Even here there is no such unintentional, unconscious process, as is customarily understood by the words "growing into."

Finally, in relation to the social process there is still another phase of the will to live which must be considered. Under certain conditions the will to live of an individual or a society can express itself only through the subjection of the will to live of other individuals. The beast of prey can live only through the destruction of other animals. Often his will to live demands the dispossession of some of his own kind who contend with him for prey, or who diminish the supply of food. This does not demand the destruction of these others, but the bending of their will because of a superiority of muscle or nerve force.

Such contests also take place among men. They are less frequent between individuals than between societies. They are waged over means of winning life, from hunting grounds and fishing places to markets and colonies. Such conflicts always end either with the destruction of one party, or, more frequently, with a breaking or bending of its will. Each time this is only a passing event. But out of this develops a continuous bending of the will of one man by another, that ends in a condition of continuous exploitation.

Class antagonisms are antagonisms of volitions. The will to live of the capitalists meets with conditions that force it to bend the will of the workers and to make use of it. Without this bending of the will there would be no capitalist profit, and no capitalist could exist. The will of the laborer to live, on the other hand, forces him to rebel against the will of the capitalist. Therefore the class struggle.

Thus we see that the will is the motive force of the whole economic process. It is the starting point and enters into every expression of that process. There is nothing more absurd than to look upon the will and economic phenomena as two factors independent of each other. It is a part of the fetish-like conception that confuses the economic process—that is, the forms of social co-operative and competitive labor of mankind—with the material objects of such labor, and that imagines that just as men make use of raw materials and tools to form certain objects according to their own ideas, so the "creative personalities" make use through their free will of the economic process to form "thus and so," certain definite social relations to suit their needs. Because the laborer stands outside of the raw material and tools, because he stands above them and rules them, these worshipers of the economic fetish, think that man stands outside the economic process, that he stands above it and rules it according to his free will.

There is no more ridiculous misunderstanding than this.

Economic necessity does not mean absence of will. It springs from the necessity of the will to live of living creatures, and from the inevitable necessity arising therefrom to utilize the conditions of life that they meet. It is the necessity of a predetermined volition.

There could also be no greater perversion of the truth than the idea that a knowledge of economic necessity means a weakening of the volition, and that the will of the workers must be aroused by biographies of generals and other powerful willed men, and by lectures on the freedom of the will. When the people have once been persuaded that a thing exists, then it must exist and can be used by them! If you do not believe this take a look at our professors and other bourgeois intellectuals, who have had a course in Kant on one side, and worshiped the powerful willed Hohenzollerns on the other, and observe what a great inflexible will they have obtained by this means.

If the will to live, which is the foundation of all economic necessity, is not most powerful in the workers, if this will must first artificially be awakened in them, then is all our struggle in vain.

This does not by any means imply that human volition has no relation to consciousness and is not determined by it. The energy of the will to live, to be sure, does not depend upon our consciousness, but our consciousness does determine the *form* that it will express itself in in any given case, and the amount of energy that the individual will expend in any given form. We have seen that next to instinct consciousness rules the will and that the way in which it is directed depends upon in what

manner and to what degree the consciousness recognizes
the conditions of existence. Since the intellect differs
with individuals it can react differently upon the same
will to live under the same conditions of life. It is this
difference that gives the appearance of freedom of the
will and makes it look as though the form of the volition
of the individual depended, not upon the conditions of
life, but upon his own will.

It is not through edifying legends and speculations
concerning the freedom of the will, but only through a
broader insight into social relations that the proletarian
will can be awakened and its energy directed into the
channels most effective for the furtherance of proletarian
interests.

The will to live is the fact from which we must always
take our start—that we must presume to exist. The form
which it takes and the intensity with which it expresses
itself depend, with each individual, class, nation, etc.,
upon their knowledge of the actual conditions of life.
Wherever two classes arise developing opposing wills,
the conditions are presented for conflict.

We have to deal only with this latter situation.

The expression of the will as the spirit of conflict is
determined by three things: First, by the *stake* for
which the combatants are striving; second, by their *consciousness of strength;* third, by their *actual strength*.

The greater the stake of battle, the stronger the will,
the more the fighters will dare, the more eager the sacrifice of every energy to attain that stake. But this
holds true only when one is convinced that the forces
at his disposal are sufficient to attain the prize. If this
necessary self-confidence is lacking, the prize may be
ever so alluring, it will still fail to release any volition,
but will only arouse desires and longings, and no matter
how intense these may be they will give birth to no actual
deed, and for all practical purposes are completely useless.

The feeling of strength is again worse than useless when it is not based upon actual knowledge of its own and its opponents' powers, but depends upon pure illusions. Strength, without a feeling of strength, is dead, and arouses no volition. A feeling of strength without strength can, under certain circumstances, lead to actions that may overwhelm or destroy an opponent, weakening or bending his will. But permanent results are not to be obtained without actual strength. Undertakings that are carried through without actual strength, but whose success depends upon deceiving an opponent as to his real strength, are doomed to failure sooner or later, and the disappointment which they will bring with them will be all the greater in proportion as their first successes were brilliant.

When we apply what has just been said to the class struggle of the proletariat it shows us what must be the nature of the work of those who would fight with and for that class and how the Socialist movement affects it. Our first and greatest task must be to increase the strength of the proletariat. Naturally we cannot increase this by wishing for it. At any definite period of capitalist society the strength of the proletariat is determined by economic conditions and cannot arbitrarily be increased. But the effect of its existing strength can be increased by preventing its waste. The unconscious processes of nature always seem extremely wasteful when looked at from the standpoint of our purposes. Nature, however, has no purposes to serve. The conscious mind of man sets purposes before him, and also shows him the way to attain these purposes without waste of strength, and with the least expenditure of purposeful energy possible.

This holds true also in the class struggle of the proletariat. To be sure, it proceeds in the beginning without the consciousness of the participants. Their conscious volition includes only their closest personal needs. The social transformations that proceed from the effort to satisfy these needs remain hidden from the fighters. As a SOCIAL process, therefore, the class struggle is for a long time an unconscious process. As such it is laden with all the waste of energy inherent in all unconscious processes. Only through a RECOGNITION of the social process, its tendencies or aims can this waste be ended, the strength of the proletariat concentrated, the workers brought together into great organizations united upon a common aim, with all personalities and momentary actions subordinated to the permanent class interests, and those interests, in turn, placed at the service of the collective social evolution.

In other words, the theory is the factor that raises to the highest degree the strength which it is possible for the proletariat to develop. The theory does this by teaching the workers how to use the powers arising at any given stage of economic development in the most effective manner and by preventing the waste of those powers.

The theory does not simply increase the effective strength of the proletariat; it also increases the consciousness of that strength. This latter is something that is no less necessary.

We have seen that the will is determined, not alone by consciousness, but by customs and instinct. Relations that have been constantly repeated through decades, and indeed through centuries, create customs and instincts, that continue to operate after their material basis has disappeared. A class may have become weak that once ruled because of its superior strength, and a class that it exploits may become strong, that at one time was weak and permitted itself to be laden with an exploiting class. But the inherited consciousness of strength may long affect both sides until there comes a test of strength, such, for example, as a war, that exposes the whole weakness of the ruling class. Then the subject class suddenly becomes conscious of its strength and a revolution follows.

The proletariat is affected in this manner by the feeling of its original weakness and a belief in the invincibility of the capitalists.

The capitalist system of production arose in a period during which the mass of the proletariat had been thrown upon the street to a parasitic, socially useless existence. The capitalist who took them into his service was their savior, their "giver of bread," or, as we say today, "giver of work," a phrase that does not sound much better. Their will to live drove them to sell themselves. They saw no possibility of existence besides this, and much less any possibility of resisting the capitalist.

But gradually relations changed. From a troublesome beggar, employed out of pity, the proletarian became the working class from which society lives. The personality of the capitalist, on the contrary, became more and more superfluous in the progress of production, something which the corporation and the trust made plainly evident. Because of economic necessity the wage relation became more and more a relation of power, maintained by the power of the state. But the proletariat grew to become the most numerous class in the state, and also in the army, upon which the power of the state rests. In a highly developed industrial state like Germany or England it already possesses the strength to capture the power of the state, and if the economic conditions now existed it could use the power of the state for the substitution of social industry for the present capitalist industry.

But what the proletariat lacks is a consciousness of its own strength. Only a few sections possess this consciousness. For the great mass it is still lacking. The Socialist movement does what it can to develop this consciousness. Here again it makes use of theoretical explanations, but not of these alone. More effective for the development of the consciousness of strength than any theory is always the deed. It is by its victories in the struggle against its opponents that the Socialist party most clearly demonstrates the strength of the proletariat, and thereby most effectively arouses a feeling of strength. These successes, in turn, are due to the circumstance that it is guided by a theory that makes it possible for the most consciously organized portion of the proletariat to utilize its maximum strength at any moment.

Everywhere outside the Anglo-Saxon countries the economic activity of the workers has been directed and ·assisted from the beginning by the knowledge of Socialism.

Next to these successes it has been the successful battles for parliament and in parliament that has done most to increase the strength and the feeling of strength on the part of the proletariat. Not alone through the material advantages that have been secured for some sections of the proletariat, but most of all through the fact that the propertyless, cowed and hopeless masses of the people saw here a power appear that boldly took up battle against the ruling powers, winning victory after victory, and which was itself nothing but an organization of these propertyless ones.

Therein lies the great significance of the first of May demonstrations, and battle of the ballots, as well as the battle for the ballot. These things often do not bring any important material advantage to the proletariat. Very often the gains are in no way proportionate to the sacrifices made. Nevertheless, every such victory signifies a mighty increase in the effective strength of the proletariat, because they mightily arouse its feeling of strength, and thereby the energy of its volition for the class struggle.

There is nothing that our opponents fear more than

this increase in the feeling of strength. They know that the giant is not dangerous to them so long as he is not conscious of his own strength. To keep down this feeling of strength is their greatest care, even material concessions are much less hated by them than moral victories of the working class, which increase its self-confidence. Therefore they often fight much harder to maintain autocratic management of the factory, to maintain the right to "run their own business," than against increases in wages. This explains the bitter enmity to the celebration of Mayday as a holiday taken by labor, and also explains the efforts to throttle universal and equal suffrage wherever it has become a means of visibly demonstrating to the population the continuous victorious advance of the Socialist party. It is not the fear of a Socialist majority that drives them to such efforts—they need not fear that for many an election.

No, it is the fear that the continual electoral victories of the Socialists will give the proletariat such a feeling of strength, and so overawe its opponents that it will be impossible to prevent the seizure of the powers of the state and the transformation of the relation of powers in the government.

Consequently we must be prepared to see our next great electoral victory followed by an attack on the present suffrage law for the Reichstag elections—by which I do not by any means say that this attack will be successful.

To be sure, our party does not have victories alone to record, but defeats as well. But the discouraging effect of these are lessened just in proportion as we turn our attention from the local and momentary limitations to follow our movement as a whole during the last two generations in all the nations of the world. The continuous and rapid advance of the whole proletariat, in spite of very heavy individual defeats, then becomes so notorious

that nothing can destroy our confidence in ultimate
victory.

The more, however, we seek to consider our individual
battles in their relation to the whole social evolution, the
clearer and stronger we keep before us the freeing of
the working class, and thereby of all mankind from all
class domination as the final object of all our endeavors,
the more our minor tasks are enobled, the more continuously and impressively the will to live on the part of
the proletariat expresses itself, the more will the great-
ness of the battle prize spur that will on to the greatest
possible revolutionary passion, that is not the product
of a senseless excitement, but of clear and definite
knowledge.

These are the methods by which Socialism has aroused
the volition of the working class up to the present time,
and this has produced such marvelous results that there
is not the slightest reason why these methods should be
exchanged for any other.

CHAPTER V.

On the one side we Marxists are accused of having excluded the will from politics and of having thereby reduced politics to an automatic process. On the other side, these same critics assert the exact reverse. They allege that our desires far exceed our knowledge of reality. They claim that the facts should teach us the impossibility of any revolution, but that we cling to the idea of revolution out of pure sentimental fanaticism until we are drunk with it. They allege that we are seeking a political revolution at any price, even though we might progress faster on the existing legal basis. . . .

(Kautsky here introduces an argument and quotations to show that Frederick Engels did not disavow the revolutionary position, as has been sometimes claimed. This matter deals so largely with German local politics as to be of little interest to English readers.)

I discussed this question of the revolution in the Neuen Zeit in December, 1893, and I will simply reproduce a portion of what was said there.

We are revolutionists, and this not simply in the sense that the steam engine is a revolutionist. The social transformation for which we are striving can be attained only through a political revolution, by means of the conquest of political power by the fighting proletariat. The only form of the state in which Socialism can be realized

49

is that of a republic, and a thoroughly democratic republic at that.

The Socialist party is a revolutionary party, but not a
revolution-making party. We know that our goal can be
attained only through a revolution. We also know that
it is just as little in our power to create this revolution
as it is in the power of our opponents to prevent it. It
is no part of our work to instigate a revolution or to
prepare the way for it. And since the revolution cannot
be arbitrarily created by us, we cannot say anything whatever about when, under what conditions, or what forms
it will come. We know that the class struggle between
the bourgeoisie and the proletariat cannot end until the
latter is in full possession of the political powers and has
used them to introduce the Socialist society. We know
that this class struggle must grow both extensively and
intensively. We know that the proletariat must continue
to grow in numbers and to gain in moral and economic
strength, and that therefore its victory and the overthrow
of capitalism is inevitable. But we can have only the
vaguest conjectures as to when and how the last decisive
blows in the social war will be struck. All this is nothing
new. . . .

Since we know nothing concerning the decisive battles
of the social war, we are manifestly unable to say whether
they will be bloody or not, whether physical force will
play a decisive part, or whether they will be fought exclusively by means of economic, legislative and moral
pressure.

We are, however, quite safe in saying that in all prob-
ability the revolutionary battles of the proletariat will see
a much greater predominance of these latter methods
over physical, which means military force, than was the
case in the revolutionary battles of the bourgeoisie.

The one reason why the battles of the coming revolution will be less frequently fought out by military

methods is to be found in the fact, which has been often pointed out, of the colossal superiority of the weapons of the present standing armies, as compared with the weapons in the possession of civilians, and which makes any resistance of the latter practically doomed to failure from the beginning.

On the other hand the revolutionary sections of today have better weapons for economic, political and moral resistance than was at the disposal of the revolutionaries of the eighteenth century. Russia is the only exception to this rule.

Freedom of organization and of the press and universal suffrage (under certain circumstances universal military duty) not only place weapons in the hands of the proletariat of modern nations which give them an advantage over the classes which fought the revolutionary battles of the bourgeoisie; these institutions shed a light upon the relative strength of the various parties and classes and upon the spirit that animates them, and this light was wholly lacking under absolutism.

At that time the ruling classes as well as the revolutionary ones were groping about in the dark. Since every expression of opposition was rendered impossible neither the government nor the revolutionists could gain any idea of their strength. Each party was in danger of overestimating its strength so long as it had not measured it against an opponent. It was, on the other hand, inclined to underestimate it as soon as it suffered the slightest defeat.

This is one of the principal reasons why, during the bourgeoisie revolutions, so many uprisings were suppressed with a single blow, and why so many governments were overthrown at a single stroke, and why revolution was so generally followed by a counter revolution.

It is wholly different today in those countries having any democratic institutions. Such institutions have been

called social safety valves. If this expression is intended
to mean that in a democracy the proletariat ceases to be
revolutionary, and that it is satisfied with a public expression of its anger and its sufferings, and that it re-
nounces the political and social revolution, then the expression is false. Democracy cannot do away with the
class antagonisms of capitalist society. Neither can it
avoid the final outcome of these antagonisms—the overthrow of present society. One thing it can do. It cannot
abolish the revolution, but it can avert many premature,
hopeless revolutionary attempts, and render superfluous
many revolutionary uprisings. It creates clearness regarding the relative strength of the different parties and
classes. It does not abolish their antagonisms, nor postpone their ultimate object, but it does operate to hinder
the rising class from sometimes attempting the accomplishment of tasks of which it is not yet capable, and to
keep the governing class from refusing concessions that
it no longer possesses the strength to maintain. The
direction of development is not thereby changed, but its
course becomes steadier and more peaceful.

The advance of the proletariat in those nations with
some democratic institutions is not marked by such striking victories as those of the bourgeoisie during its time
of revolution; but it also lacks the great defeats. Since
the appearance of the modern Socialist labor movement
in the '6os, the European proletariat has met with but
one great defeat—that of the Commune of 1871. At
that time France was suffering from the victories of
the German empire, that had withheld democratic institutions from its people, while the French proletariat had
attained to but the dawn of class consciousness and was
forced into the uprising.

The democratic-proletarian method of battle may appear more monotonous than the revolutionary period of
the bourgeoisie; it is certainly less dramatic and striking,

but it calls for far fewer sacrifices. This may be somewhat disappointing to those smart literary persons who
come to Socialism as an interesting sport, looking for interesting stuff, but not to those who actually have to do
the fighting.*

These so-called peaceful methods of conducting the
class struggle, which are confined to non-military measures (parliamentarism, strikes, demonstrations, the press
and similar methods of bringing pressure to bear) stand
a chance of being maintained in any country the more
democratic the institutions, and the greater the political
and economic insight and the self control of the people.

Of two opponents confronted with the same conditions,
that one is most likely to retain his cool-headedness who
feels himself superior to the other. On the contrary, the
person who does not have faith in his own ability quickly
becomes excited and loses his self-control.

In all civilized countries it is the proletariat above all
other classes that has the greatest faith in itself and its
cause. It is not necessary for it to cultivate any illusions
for this purpose. It need only study the history of the
last generation, to see how it has moved forward everywhere uninterruptedly. It has only to trace the course
of evolution in present society to be convinced that its
victory is inevitable. It is not, therefore, to be expected
that in those countries where it is most highly developed,
the proletariat will easily lose its head and its self-control

---

* "Capitalist revolutions, like those of the eighteenth century,
rush swiftly on from victory to victory, their dramatic effects pile
climax upon climax, men and things appear in most glowing bril-
liancy, ecstasy becomes the every-day spirit; but they are short-
lived, they soon reach their apex and there is a long 'morning
after' (katzenjammer), for society, before the results of the storm
and stress period are deliberately appropriated. Proletarian revolutions, on the contrary, .   .   .   are constantly criticizing themselves, etc." (Marx, "The Eighteenth Brumaire.") In the comparison which he made in 1852, between the capitalist and proletarian revolution, Marx naturally did not take into consideration
the influence of democratic institutions.

and enter upon any adventurous policy. And the danger
of this is lessened just in proportion to the simultaneous
height of culture, the insight of the working class and
the democratic development of the state.

On the other hand, the same assurance cannot be of-
fered in regard to the ruling class. It sees and feels that
it is growing weaker from day to day and is accordingly
more and more nervous and uneasy, and consequently
uncertain. It is more and more approaching a state of
mind where it is evident that it is liable to be seized with
a fit of desperate rage that will lead it to throw itself
furiously upon its opponent, in a desperate hope of gaining a victory regardless of the wounds it may inflict upon
the whole social body, and also of the irreparable destruction it may produce.

The political situation of the proletariat is such that it
can well afford to try as long as possible to progress
through strictly "legal" methods alone. The danger that
these efforts to progress peacefully will be thwarted lies
principally in just this nervous attitude of the ruling
class.

The statesmen of the ruling class desire above everything else the commission of some insane act that would
arouse, not only the ruling class itself, but the whole
great indifferent mass of the population against the Socialists, and they desire this before the Socialists shall
have become too powerful to be defeated. Such an oc-
currence offers the only possible hope of putting off the
victory of the working class for at least a number of
years. To be sure, they are staking everything on this
game. If it is not successful and the proletariat is not
overthrown in the act of rage that follows, then the collapse of the capitalist class will but be hastened, and the
triumph of Socialism be brought so much nearer. But
the politicians of the ruling class have reached a condition where they are ready to risk everything upon a single

throw of the dice. They would rather take their chances in a civil war than endure the fear of a revolution.

The Socialists, on the other hand, not only have no reason to follow suit in this policy of desperation, but should much rather seek by every means in their power to postpone any such insane uprising, even if it is recognized as inevitable, to a time when the proletariat shall be so powerful as to be able to at once whip the enraged mob and to restrain it so that the one paroxysm shall be its last, and the destruction that it brings and the sacrifice it costs shall be as small as possible.

The Socialists must, therefore, avoid, and indeed actively oppose, any purposeless provocation of the ruling class that might give their statesmen an opportunity to rouse a mad rage against the Socialists. When we declare that revolutions cannot be made, and when we maintain that it is foolish, and indeed pernicious to incite to revolution, and when we act in accordance with these statements, we do not do this in the interest of the capitalist politicians, but of the fighting proletariat. These same tactics have been followed by the Socialist parties of all countries. Because of this fact the ruling class politicians have not, as yet, been able to accomplish what they have desired.

Although the political influence of the Socialists is as yet comparatively small, still it is, in most modern states, too great for the capitalist politicians to do with it as they desire. Petty measures and punishments do not help them; they merely embitter those against whom they are directed, without either frightening them or diminishing their combativeness. Every attempt to carry out such unfair measures for the purpose of disarming the proletariat, carries with it the danger of civil war, which, whatever its final outcome might be, is sure to bring terrible devastation. Everyone with even a little foresight knows this.

However anxious capitalist politicians may be to drive the Socialists to a test of strength, which they are not yet, perhaps, strong enough to meet, the capitalist business men have no desire to enter upon an experiment that may easily ruin any one of them. They certainly will not invite anything of the kind so long as they retain their judgment and are not carried away by any attack of insane rage such as has already been discussed.

The interest of the proletariat today more than ever before demands that everything should be avoided that would tend to provoke the ruling class to a purposeless policy of violence. The Socialist party governs itself in accord with this position.

There is, however, a faction that calls itself proletarian and social revolutionary which takes as its most favored task, next to fighting the Socialist party, the provoking of a policy of violence. The very thing that the statesmen of the ruling class desire, and which is alone capable of checking the victorious progress of the proletariat, is made the principal business of this faction, thereby gaining them the special favor of Puttkamer and his followers. The adherents of this faction do not seek to WEAKEN but to ENRAGE the capitalist.

The overthrow of the Paris Commune was, as has already been noted, the last great defeat of the proletariat. Since that time it has, in most countries, marched steadily forward. This has been due to the acceptance of the tactics just described, and if the progress has sometimes been slower than we might desire, it has been more certain than that of any previous revolutionary movement.

There have been but few instances since 1871 where the proletarian movement has suffered any setback, and in every instance these have been due to the interference by individuals with methods that we have come to designate as "anarchistic," since they correspond to the tactics

preached by the great majority of present-day anarchists
as the "propaganda of the deed."

Concerning the evils inflicted by the anarchists in the
"International" and by the uprising in Spain in 1873 we
can only make a passing reference. Five years after these
uprisings came the incident of the popular rage excited
by the attacks of Hodel and Nobiling, without which Bismarck would scarcely have been able to carry his anti-
Socialist laws. It certainly could not have been so rigor-
ously administered as it was during the first years of its
existence, and the German proletariat would have been
spared some terrible sacrifices, and its victorious progress
would not have been checked even for a moment.

The next setback suffered by the labor movement was
in Austria in 1884 as a result of the knavery and bes-
tiality of Kammerer, Stellmacher, and their followers.
The mightily growing Socialist movement there was overthrown at a single stroke without being able to offer a
trace of resistance, crushed, not by the authorities, but
by the general rage of the people, who charged the
Socialists with the acts of the so-called anarchists.

Another setback came in America in 1886. The labor
movement had been growing rapidly, and had attained
great power. It had been progressing with such giant
strides that many observers thought it possible that within
a short time it would pass the European movement and
stand on the apex of the labor movement of the world.
In the spring of 1886 the unions made a tremendous
concerted effort to secure the eight hour day. The labor
organizations grew to colossal size. Strike followed
strike. The most hopeful expectations ruled, and the
Socialists, always the foremost and most active, began to
attain to the leadership of the movement.

Then at one of the numerous clashes between the
laborers and the police came the well known Chicago
bomb affair of May 4. No one knows, even today, who

was the real author of this affair. The anarchists who were hung upon the 11th of November and their associates, who were condemned to long terms of imprisonment, were the sacrifices of a judicial murder. But the deed had corresponded to the tactics so long preached by the anarchists. It released the rage of the entire bourgeoisie of America, confused the laborers and discredited the Socialists, whom the people did not know how to distinguish from the anarchists, and whom they often did not wish to distinguish.

The struggle for the eight hour day ended with the defeat of the workers. The labor movement collapsed and the Socialist movement sank into insignificance. Not until within recent years has it once more slowly arisen in the United States.

The only great injuries suffered by the labor movement during the last twenty years have come as a result of acts for which the anarchists were directly responsible, or else which were in accord with the tactics they preach. The anti-Socialist laws of Germany, the exceptional conditions in Austria, the judicial murder in Chicago, with its results, all were thereby made possible.

The possibility that anarchy will again gain a hold upon the masses, is today much less than ever before.

The two great causes which made the people receptive to anarchy were lack of insight and hopelessness, and especially the apparent impossibility of securing the slightest improvement by means of political action.

During the first half of the '80s, during the time when the laborers of Austria and the United States were captured by anarchistic phrases, both countries showed a most remarkable growth in the labor movement—but which was also almost entirely without leaders. The battalions of labor were formed almost entirely from undrilled recruits, without knowledge, without experience and without officers. And out of this condition arose the apparent impossibility of overthrowing the political domination of capital by political methods. The laborers of Austria did not possess the suffrage and had little hopes of obtaining it through legal methods in any conceivable time. In America the laborers were disheartened by the political corruption.

Even in other countries beside these two there was a pessimistic wave during the '8os.

Since then things have changed everywhere for the better.

In Austria there was still another condition favoring the rise of anarchy—*faith in the Socialists had been almost destroyed among the masses.* When the political and economic weapons—the organization and the press—of the German proletariat were destroyed by the anti-Socialist laws, the just arising anarchists in Austria took advantage of this situation to accuse the party which had thus been rendered momentarily dumb, of having thrown away its weapons and renounced its revolutionary principles. The Austrian Socialists who defended their German comrades not only failed to rehabilitate the latter in the eyes of the majority of the Austrian laborers, but only succeeded in discrediting themselves. A government official, Count Lamezan, gave his assistance to the anarchists, who were naturally very much beloved by him, and sneeringly declared that the Socialists were only "revolutionists in dressing gowns."

Even today the anarchists devote most of their activities to showing that the Socialists are only "revolutionists in dressing gowns."

Up to the present time they have had little success. But if it should ever be possible for an anarchist movement to gain a foothold in Germany, it would not be because of the agitation of the "independents," but either through such action of the ruling class as would destroy all hope among the laborers and inspire them with an attitude of

extreme prejudice, or else through events among ourselves which would arouse the idea that we had relinquished our revolutionary attitude. The more "moderate"
we become, therefore, the more water we supply to the
mills of the anarchists, and thus give aid to just the
movement that would substitute the most brutal forms of
battle for the civilized forms of struggle. We may say
that there is today one force that would cause the workers
to turn of their own accord from the "peaceable" methods
of struggles that we have just been considering—the loss
of faith in the revolutionary character of our party. We
can endanger the course of peaceful evolution only by
too great peacefulness.

We do not need to state here what misfortunes will
follow any wavering in our policy.

The opposition of the possessing classes will not
thereby be diminished, and no trustworthy friends will
be won thereby. It would, however, introduce confusion
into our own ranks, render the indifferent more indifferent still and drive away the energetic.

The greatest force making for our success is the revolutionary enthusiasm. We will need this more in the
future than ever before, for the greatest difficulties are
before, not behind us. So much the worse for all these
things that tend to weaken this power.

The present situation brings the danger that we will
appear more "moderate" than we really are. The
stronger we become the more practical tasks are forced
into the foreground, the more we must extend our agitation beyond the circle of the industrial wage worker,
and just so much the more we are compelled to guard
against any useless provocation or any absolutely empty
threats. It is very difficult to maintain the proper bal-
ance, to give the present its full due without losing sight
of the future, to enter into the mental attitude of the
farmers and the small capitalists without giving up the

proletarian standpoint, to avoid all possible provocation and yet always maintain the consciousness that we are a fighting party, conducting an irreconcilable war upon all existing social institutions.

The above paragraphs were written in 1893. They also contain a prophecy that has since been fulfilled. What I feared in 1893 appeared a few years later. In France a portion of our party membership became temporarily a government party. The masses received the impression that the Socialists had renounced their revolutionary principles. They lost faith in the party. Not a small section of them fell under the influence of the latest variety of anarchism—syndicalism—which, like the old anarchism, follows the propaganda of the deed not so much to strengthen the proletariat as unnecessarily to frighten the bourgeoisie, to arouse its rage and provoke immature, inopportune tests of strength, to which the proletariat is not adequate in the existing conditions.

It is just the revolutionary Marxists among French Socialists who have presented the most determined opposition to this tendency. They fight syndicalism as energetically as ministerialism, and consider one just as injurious as the other.

The revolutionary Marxists are still standing today upon the standpoint developed by Engels and myself in the articles just quoted, written in 1892-1895.

We are neither men of legality at any price, nor are we revolutionists at any price. We know that we cannot create historical situations to suit our desires, and that our tactics must correspond to such situations.

At the beginning of the '90s I had recognized that further peaceful development of the proletarian organizations and the proletarian class struggle, upon the then existing governmental foundations, would best advance the proletariat in the situation existing at that time. Neither can I be accused of being drunk with r-r-revolution and r-r-radicalism when my observation of the present situation leads me to the conclusion that the situation which existed at the beginning of the '90s has fundamentally changed, and that today we have every reason to believe that we are entering upon a period of fighting for governmental institutions and governmental power; that these battles under manifold conditions and changes of fortune may continue for a decade, and that the form and duration of these battles cannot now be foretold, but which it is highly probable will within a comparatively short time bring about important changes in relative power in favor of the proletariat, if they do not bring its complete domination in Western Europe.

The reasons for these views will be indicated in the following chapters.

CHAPTER VI.

THE GROWTH OF REVOLUTIONARY ELEMENTS.

We have seen that the Marxists have shown themselves to be by no means as poor prophets as some people would like to make them appear. Many of them, to be sure, have been wrong in some ONE point, as, for example, the setting of a date for the great revolutionary struggle that shall bring about important political alterations of power in the interest of the proletariat.

What reason have we to expect that now, at last, the long expected time is drawing close when the ban of political stagnation will be broken, and that once more the fresh, joyful life of battle and victorious progress on the road to political power will appear?

In his introduction to Marx's "Class Struggles in France," to which reference has already been made, Engels quite properly pointed out that, under present conditions, a great revolutionary struggle can be carried on only by great masses who know what they intend to do. The times are past in which a small minority, by a sudden energetic action, can overthrow a government and erect a new one in its place.

This was possible in a centralized state where all political power was concentrated in a capital city which dominated the entire country, and where the villages and smaller cities had no trace of political life and no power of co-operation. Whoever was able to cripple the military forces and the bureaucracy of the capital, or to win it to their side, could seize the powers of government,

63

and, if the general conditions were favorable to a social revolution, use them for that purpose.

Today, in the age of railroads and telegraphs, of newspapers and public assemblages, of countless industrial centers, of magazine rifles and machine guns, it is absolutely impossible for a minority to cripple the military forces of the capital, unless they are already completely disorganized. It is also impossible to confine a political struggle to the capital. Political life has become national.

Where these conditions exist a great transfer of political power that shall destroy a tyrannical regime is only to be expected where all of the following conditions exist:

1. The great mass of the people must be decisively hostile to such a regime.

2. There must be a great organized party in irreconcilable opposition to such a regime.

3. This party must represent the interests of the great majority of the population and possess their confidence.

4. Confidence in the ruling regime, both in its power and in its stability, must have been destroyed by its own tools, by the bureaucracy and the army.

During the last decade, at least in Western Europe, these conditions have never existed simultaneously. For a long time the proletariat did not form a majority of the population and the Socialist Party was not the strongest party. When in previous decades we looked for the early appearance of the revolution, it was because we calculated, not alone upon the proletariat, but also upon the small capitalist democracy to help make up the mass of the revolutionary party, and upon the small capitalists and the farmers to form a party of the masses that would stand behind such a revolution. But the small capitalist democracy has completely failed in this respect. In Germany it no longer constitutes an opposition party.

On the other hand, however, the uncertainty as to conditions which prevailed in 1870 has disappeared in the great cities of Europe outside of Russia. . The government have entrenched themselves and grown in strength and security. They have learned how to gain the confidence of the mass of the nation and to convince it that they stand for its interest.

So it was that in the first decade of the rise of a permanent and independent labor movement, during the '60s of the last century, the possibilities of revolution were constantly less. At the same time the proletariat was ever in more and more need of such a revolution, and, because of the example of the decades just passed, believed such a revolution near.

But gradually conditions changed to favor its coming. The *organization of the proletariat* grew. Perhaps this was most striking in Germany. During the last dozen years this growth has been especially rapid. We have seen the organization of the Social Democrats reach a *half million members.* Closely united to it in spirit is a trade union movement with *two million* members. Simultaneously has grown its *press* as a work of the organization and not of private enterprise. The political daily press now has a circulation of nearly a *million,* and the trade union press, composed mostly of weekly papers, reaches an even greater number.

That is an organized power of the laboring subject masses such as the world has never seen before.

The domination of the ruling class over the subject class has hitherto rested in no small degree on its control of the organized means of governmental power, while the subject class was almost wholly without organization, at least of any organization extending over the field of the entire state. The working class has never been wholly without organization. Through antiquity and the middle ages and up to recent times these organizations, however,

were confined either to single, narrow BRANCHES OF IN-
DUSTRY or to single, narrow LOCALITIES—either guild or
municipal corporations.

Under certain circumstances these could exercise a
strong restraint over municipalities. There can be no
greater mistake than to confuse state and community
without distinguishing between them, and to designate
one and the other as organizations of the same class
domination. A community CAN be, and often is, the same
as the state. A community, within the state, may also
represent the subject class, if this constitutes a majority
and asserts itself. During the last century it performed
this function in the most striking manner in the municipality of Paris. This municipality came to be the organization of the lowest classes of society.

But in no great state of today is it possible for a single
municipality to maintain its independence in opposition
to the power of the state. It is therefore all the more
necessary that the subject classes should be organized
in great organizations extending over the entire scope
of the state and embracing all branches of industry.

This has been most successfully accomplished in Germany. Not only in France, but also in England with
its old trade unions, is the economic as well as the political movement very much divided. But however much
the proletarian organizations may grow, they will never
in normal, non-revolutionary times include the whole of
the laboring class within the state, but only an elite, that
through either trade, local or individual peculiarities are
raised above the mass of the population. On the other
hand, the attractive power of a class organization in
revolutionary times, in which even the weakest feel themselves capable of and willing to fight, depends upon the
numerical strength of the classes whose interests it rep-
resents.

It is therefore noteworthy that the wage workers con-

stitute a majority, not only of the POPULATION, but even
of the electorate, in the German Empire.

The exact figures of the laboring population from the
census of 1907 are not yet available. We must therefore
take those for 1895. When we compare these with the
election of 1893 we obtain the following:

In 1893 the number entitled to vote was 10,628,292.
On the other hand, there were in 1895 15,506,482 persons active in industry. Subtract from this figure the
number of those under twenty years of age, and one-
half of those between twenty and thirty, and we have
10,742,989, as the nearest figure obtainable of the male
industrial workers of voting age. This number is almost
identical with the number of those entitled to vote in
1893.

Of the male industrial workers of voting age in agriculture, industry and trade (reckoned in the same manner) there were again 4,172,269 independent producers
and 5,590,743 wage workers and salary force. If we consider, however, that in business (trade and industry)
alone, that of the 3,144,977 heads of business more than
one-half, 1,714,351, a single person was both employer
and employe, and that therefore the overwhelming majority of these fall within the circle of interest of the
proletariat, then we are not exaggerating when we accept
the statement that in 1895, while there were three and a
half million such "independent" producers who were interested in private property in the means of production,
there were more than six million proletarians who were
interested in the abolition of this private property.

We may take it for granted that in the remaining
strata of the population that are to be considered, while
insignificant in numbers, is divided in about the same
way. This is especially true of those who are classified
as "independent without occupation," and who are composed upon the one side of rich capitalist landlords and

on the other of needy invalids and recipients of old-age pensions.

If we take the total population engaged in productive industry, the preponderance of the proletariat is much greater than among those entitled to the suffrage. Those active in industry who do not vote are nearly all child laborers.

The figures are as follows:

Age.	Independent.	Employes.
18-20 years	42,711	1,335,016
20-30 years	613,045	3,935,592
On the other hand:		
30-40 years	1,319,201	3,111,115
40-50 years	1,368,261	1,489,317
Over 50 years...............	2,102,814	1,648,085

Altogether in agriculture, industry and trade there are 5,474,046 "independents" and 13,438,377 employes. If we deduct from this first class a portion composed of home workers, and similar "independents" who are really disguised proletarians, we can safely say that in 1895 scarcely _one-fourth_ of the productive population was interested in the maintenance of private property in the means of production, while the proletariat composed fully one-third of the electorate.

Thirteen years earlier, in 1882, the conditions were not yet so favorable. If we compare the figures of the occupation statistics of 1882 with those of the election of 1881, and use the same method of calculation we have just applied to the figures for 1895, we obtain the following:

Year.	Total Voters.	Voters.	Voting Laborers.
1882	9,090,381	3,947,192	4,744,021
1895	10,628,292	4,172,269	5,590,743
Increase	1,537,911	225,077	846,722

The number of individual industries was almost as great in 1882 as in 1895—1,877,872. But the number of those classified as "independent" who led a non-proletarian existence was certainly higher in 1882 than in 1895. We can also certainly take it for granted that the number of those interested in the maintenance of private property in the instruments of production was proportionately greater in 1882 than in 1895, when it was in the neighborhood of three and one-half million. The proletarian element, on the contrary, included about five million. The defenders of private property have, therefore, remained practically the same from 1882 to 1895. The number of their opponents in the electorate, on the contrary, has increased a million.

The number of Socialist votes grew at an even more rapid rate during this period, increasing from 311,901 to 1,780,989. To be sure, the number of Socialist votes in 1881 was artificially decreased by the anti-Socialist laws.

Since 1895 capitalist development, and with it the growth of the proletariat, has made yet greater progress. Unfortunately the statistics of 1907 that would give us the desired enlightenment on these points are not yet available for the whole empire.

According to some preliminary statements the number of male "independent persons" in agriculture, industry and trade, during the period from 1895 to 1907 increased but 33,084—practically not at all. The number of male clerical workers and wage workers, the proletariat, increased 2,891,228, or almost a hundred times as much.

The proletarian element that in 1895 was already the dominant element in the population and in the electorate, has since then enormously increased its preponderance.

If we take it for granted that the proportion of those entitled to suffrage among the "independents" and the laborers remained the same as in 1895, then we can carry forward the table already given in the following manner:

Year.	Total Voters.	"Independent" Voters.	Laboring Voters.
1895	10,628,292	4,172,269	5,590,743
1908	13,352,900	4,202,903	7,275,944
Increase	2,724,608	30,634	1,685,201

The lion's share of the increase in the number of voters falls to the proletariat and this in a higher degree than in the period from 1882 to 1895.

The figures of the census of 1905 are also strikingly significant as showing industrial progress.

As a general thing the cities are much more favorable to the political life and organization of the proletariat and to the extension of our teachings than the open country. It is therefore highly significant that the population of the latter has retreated before that of the cities.

How swiftly this change is proceeding is shown by the following table. The country population includes all those living in communities having less than 2,000 population, and the city population those living in communities of more than 2,000.

Year.	—Rural Population— Number.	Per Cent.	—City Population— Number.	Per Cent.
1871	26,219,352	63.9	14,790,798	36.1
1880	26,513,531	58.6	18,720,530	41.4
1890	26,185,241	53.0	23,243,229	47.0
1900	25,734,103	45.7	30,633,075	54.3
1905	25,822,481	42.6	34,818,797	57.4

In a period of thirty years the city population has more than *doubled*, while the country population has not only relatively but *absolutely* decreased. While the city dwellers have increased more than twenty millions, the number living in the country has decreased nearly one million. At the time of the establishment of the German empire the latter formed almost two-thirds of the population; today they form but a little over two-fifths.

So the economic development operates to continuously

increase the revolutionary element among the people, that element that is interested in the abolition of the present property and political institutions, and to give it a greater preponderance in the state, and this at the expense of the *sic* conservative elements.

To be sure, these revolutionary elements are only revolutionary as a *possibility*, not as a *reality*. They constitute the recruiting ground for the "soldiers of the revolution," but not all are at once such soldiers.

To a large degree hatched out of the small capitalist and small farmer class, many proletarians long carry the shells of these classes about with them. They do not feel themselves proletarians, but as would-be property owners. They live in the hope of getting a little strip of land, or of opening a miserable little store, or of becoming "independent" by establishing a tiny hand industry with a couple of unfortunate apprentices. Others have given up hope in these directions, or recognize what a miserable existence these things really mean, but they are still unwilling to fight for a better existence in co-operation with their comrades. Such become strike breakers and yellow trade unionists. Others, again, have gone further, and have come to recognize the necessity of fighting the capitalists that stand in antagonism to them, but do not feel themselves secure enough and strong enough to declare war upon the entire capitalist system. These look to capitalist parties and governments for relief.

Indeed, even among those who have become thoroughly conscious of the necessity of the proletarian class struggle, there are still plenty who cannot escape from the influence of present society, and who doubt or despair of the victory of the proletariat.

Just so much the more rapid the economic development, and therewith the proletarianization of the population proceeds, the more numerous the hordes that stream from the country to the city, from the East to the West, out of the ranks of the small possessors into the ranks of propertyless, just so much the more numerous within the ranks of the proletarians is the element that have not yet comprehended the significance of the social revolution, indeed that do not even understand the significance of the class antagonisms in our society.

To win these to the idea of Socialism is an indispensable, but, under ordinary conditions, a very difficult task, that demands the greatest sacrifice and skill, and never proceeds as fast as we wish. Our recruiting ground today includes fully *three-fourths* of the population, probably even more; the number of votes that are given to us do not equal *one-third* of all the voters, and not *one-fourth* of all those entitled to vote.

But the rate of progress increases with a leap when the revolutionary spirit is abroad. It is almost inconceivable with what rapidity the mass of the people reach a clear consciousness of their class interests at such a time. Not alone their courage and their belligerency, but their political interest as well, is spurred on in the highest degree through the consciousness that the hour has at last come for them to burst out of the darkness of night into the glory of the full glare of the sun. Even the laziest becomes industrious, even the most cowardly becomes brave, and even the most narrow gains a wider view. In such times a single year will accomplish an education of the masses that would otherwise have required a generation.

When such a situation has arisen, when a stage has been reached where internal conflicts threaten a collapse, and if there is within such a nation a class that is interested in attaining, and has the power to take political power, then the only thing that is needed is a party that possesses the confidence of this class, and which stands in irreconcilable antagonism to the tottering regime, and which clearly recognizes the existing situation, in order to lead the aspiring class to victory.

The Socialist party has long been such a party. The revolutionary class is also here, and has for some time constituted a majority of the nation. Can we also reckon upon the moral collapse of the ruling regime?

CHAPTER VII.

THE SOFTENING OF CLASS ANTAGONISMS.

We have seen how Engels in 1885 called attention to the fact that since the French Revolution, with its after effects, which continued from 1789 to 1815, revolution had come in Europe in periods of about fifteen years—in 1815, 1830, 1848-52, 1870-71. From this Engels concluded that the next revolution was due about the close of the '80s or the beginning of the '90s. There actually was a great political transformation about this time, culminating in the overthrow of the Bismarckian regime and a revival of democratic and social-reform efforts throughout all Europe. But this uprising was insignificant and short lived, and since then almost two decades have passed without any actual revolution taking place—at least in Europe proper.

Why is this? How are we to account for the continuous unrest in Europe from 1789 to 1871, and for the continuous stability in political conditions since, which has now culminated in complete political stagnation?

During the whole of the first half of the nineteenth century large sections of the population, of greatest importance in the economic and intellectual life, were completely excluded from the government, which, as the agent of the nobility and the priesthood, was in sharp opposition to them, partly through misunderstanding and partly through direct antagonism. In Germany and Italy economic growth was prevented by the multitude of little states. The period from 1846 to 1870 greatly changed

this situation.   During this time industrial capital gained
a victory over landed property, first in England, where
the corn laws were abolished in 1846 and free trade introduced.   Elsewhere, as in Germany and Austria, industrial capital at least obtained an equal position alongside
of the landed interests.   The intellectuals secured freedom of press and movement.   The small capitalists and
farmers obtained the suffrage.   The national unity of
Germany and Italy satisfied a long-felt and urgent longing of these nations.   To be sure, this was brought about
after the collapse of the revolution of 1848, not by internal movements, but by external wars.   The Crimean War
of 1854-56 overthrew serfdom in Russia and compelled
consideration of the industrial bourgeoisie by the government of the Czar.   1859, 1866, and 1870 saw the com-
pletion of Italian unity, and 1866 and 1870 saw the same
thing accomplished in an imperfect form in Germany.   A
liberal era was begun in Austria in 1866, and in Germany
also the introduction of universal suffrage paved the way
to a certain freedom of the press and of organization.
The year 1870 completed this tendency and brought
France a democratic republic.   In England an electoral
reform was carried through in 1867 granting the suffrage
to the upper circles of the working class and such of the
small capitalists as had not obtained it previously.

These steps gave all the classes in European nations,
with the exception of the proletariat, a legal foundation
upon which to base their existence.   They had obtained,
even if in a somewhat incomplete form, the things for
which they had been striving since the great Revolution.
While all their wishes were not fulfilled, and could not be
fulfilled, since the interests of various divisions of the
possessing class are frequently antagonistic, yet those who
felt their rights abridged did not feel strong enough to
fight for complete control of the state, and the things they

lacked were not important enough to make them willing
to take the risk of a revolution.

There remains but one revolutionary class in present
European society, the PROLETARIAT, and, above all, the
city proletariat. In it the revolutionary impulse still lives.

Although the carrying out of these transformations
fundamentally altered the political situation, expectations
were still widely cherished that were based upon the experiences of the years from 1789 to 1871. Reasoning
upon the experiences of centuries, the conclusion was
drawn that there would soon be another revolution. To
be sure, it was not a purely proletarian revolution that
was expected, but a combination of a small bourgeois and
proletarian revolution, but in which the proletariat, in accordance with its increased importance, would take the
lead. This was the expectation, not alone of a few
"dogma-believing Marxists," but of practical politicians
who were wholly untouched by Marxism—such, for instance, as Bismarck. When, in 1878, he considered it
necessary to call for special legislation against the Socialists, although they had at that time not drawn to themselves a half million votes, which was less than ten per
cent of the number of voters and less than six per cent of
the total number of those entitled to vote, and if he was
even then considering the desperate remedy of trying to
provoke the Socialists to street fighting before they became irresistible, such views can be explained only on the
theory that he thought the proletarian-little bourgeois
revolution at the very door.

And, in fact, there was a series of events that favored
this view, and this wholly aside from the remembrance
of the events of the previous century.

During the '70s an economic crisis broke over Europe,
more lasting and extensive than had ever been known; it
continued until the second half of the '80s. The misery
in proletarian and small capitalist circles and the discour-

agement in capitalist circles called forth by this crisis were aggravated still further by the simultaneous sharpening of competition in the means of life from America and Russia, which apparently promised to end all agricultural production in Western Europe.

The universal misery of farmers, artisans and proletarians, the dwindling confidence of the bourgeoisie, the brutal suppression of Socialist efforts—since 1871 in France, and no less in Germany and Austria since 1878—all this appeared to indicate the early approach of a catastrophe.

But the governmental institutions that had been created between 1848 and 1871 corresponded too closely to the necessities of the great mass of the population for them to collapse at this time. On the contrary, the more threatening the danger of revolution appeared, which could be only of a proletarian, anti-capitalist character, the closer the wealthy classes clung to the government.

The small capitalists and farmers, moreover, found the newly acquired political rights, and especially the ballot, very effective means for influencing the government, and of obtaining all sorts of material concessions from it. They were all the more willing to purchase help from the government by political services, the more unbearable their previous allies in political struggles became.

So it was that the widespread discontent which arose from economic depression and political oppression produced only insignificant revolutions. The most important results of these, as has already been remarked, were the overthrow of Bismarck in 1890 and, in the course of a rather violent transformation of the French constitution, the appearance of Boulangerism in France in 1889. With these even the appearance of revolutionary situations disappeared.

Just about the time of these political transformations the long industrial depression ceased. A period of most active economic improvement began, which, with few interruptions, has continued up until within recent years. The capitalists and their intellectual retainers, professors, journalists and the like, took new courage. The hand workers shared in the improvement, and even agriculture once more enjoyed a revival. It found an expanding market in the swiftly growing industrial population, especially for such products as meat or milk, which were little affected by foreign competition. It was not the agrarian tariffs that rescued European agriculture, for even free trade countries like England, Holland, Denmark shared in the rise, but it was rather the rapid upward movement of industry which came at the end of the '80s.

This upward movement was, in turn, itself a result of the rapid extension of the world market, the same extension that had sent the stream of food stuffs pouring into Europe from distant countries, and had thereby produced the agricultural crisis. This growth of the world market was due especially to the great development of railroad construction outside Western Europe.

Following is the length of the railroads in kilometers*:

	1880.	1890.	1906.	Increase 1880-1906 Per Cent.
Germany	33,634	42,869	57,376	.70
France	25,932	36,895	47,142	.82
England	28,854	32,297	37,107	.29

On the other hand, the following six countries show a remarkable increase:

Russia	22,664	32,390	70,305	.210
British India	14,772	27,316	46,642	.215
China	11	200	5,953	54.000
Japan	121	2,333	8,067	6.666
America	171,669	331,599	473,096	.176
Africa	4,607	9,386	28,193	.513

* A mile equals 1,760 yards; a kilometer equals slightly over 1,093 yards.

One sees how much greater has been the building of railroads in the new region where capitalism has been growing than in older countries since 1880, and especially since 1890.

At the same time the means of ocean transportation have grown with leaps and bounds.   The carrying weight of ocean steamers is in tons:

	1882.	1893.	1906.
German Empire.....	249,000	783,000	2,097,000 (1907)
Great Britain	3,700,000	6,183,000	9,606,514
Norway and Sweden.	140,000	392,000	1,240,000
Denmark	67,000	123,000	376,000
France ....·....	342,000	622,000	723,000
United States.......	617,000	826,000	2,077,000 (1907)
Japan	40,000	108,000	939,000

These figures reflect the tremendous extension of the world market during the last two decades, which made possible the absorption during this period of an increased mass of goods.   As a result of this fact the attention of all industrial countries was fixed upon this world market, and, naturally, as a result, upon colonial politics, as a means of extending the foreign market.   To be sure, the acquisition of new and distant markets has done very little to extend the foreign market since the '80s.   The later colonial politics of this period have been directed almost exclusively toward Africa, where alone there still remains a large extent of what the European powers call "free" land—that is, land that is not possessed by any powerful nation.

It is only necessary to refer to the foregoing table showing the progress of railroad construction to recognize how little Africa has been touched by this extension.   To be sure, the length of its railroads during the years from 1880 to 1906 has grown from 4,600 to 28,000 kilometers, but what does this signify·beside the growth in Asia during the same period from 16,000 to 88,000 and for America of from 171,000 to 473,000.   Even in Africa itself the lion's share of the railway building was not in the new colonies that have been established since the '80s, but in the old colonies and independent states, as is shown by the following table:

Length of railroads in kilometers:

	1880.	1890.	1906.
Algeria	1,405	3,104	4,906
Egypt	1,449	1,547	5,252
Abyssinia	.....	.....	306
Cape Colony	1,457	2,922	5,812
Natal	158	546	1,458
Transvaal	...	120	2,191
Orange State	...	237	1,283
Remainder of Africa	438	919	6,985
Totals	4,607	9,356	28,193

Only 7,000 kilometers, one-fourth of the railroad mileage of Africa, less than even one per cent of the railroads of the earth, was constructed in those districts which, to be sure not all but in large part, have been acquired through the recent colonial politics of the great European powers. It is evident how little this colonial policy has had to do with the extension of the world market which has taken place during the last twenty years, or with the revival of production.

But this revival is very plainly connected with the opening of foreign markets, which has taken place simultaneously with the development of modern colonial policy since the '80s. Consequently the mass of the bourgeoisie connect the colonial policy with the improvement in economic conditions. The result is that a new ideal has arisen for the bourgeoisie of the great European powers. During the '90s this ideal began to be placed in opposition to Socialism, the same Socialism that had captured so many of the thinkers of this same bourgeoisie a decade before. This ideal was the linking together of transoceanic territory with the European government the so-called IM-PERIALISM.

The imperialism of one great nation, however, implies a policy of conquest, and implies enmity toward the other great powers which have entered upon the same policy of conquest in the same transoceanic fields. Such a policy cannot be carried out without great military preparations, without great standing armies, without fleets, that shall be in a condition to carry on battles in distant oceans.

Until the '60s the capitalist class was generally hostile to militiarism, because it was hostile to the government. It hated the standing army that cost such vast sums of money and was the strongest support of a government that was hostile to it. The capitalist democracy looked upon the standing army as superfluous, since it confined its endeavors to national boundaries, and had no wish for wars of conquest.

Since the '70s the sympathy of the capitalist class for standing armies has steadily increased, and this not alone in Germany and France, where the war of 1870 had made the army popular—in Germany as the bringer of brilliant victories, in France as a means of avoiding such desolation as that war had brought. In other countries also there began to be enthusiasm for the standing army, as much as a means of repressing the internal enemy as of repulsing external foes. The possessing class became friendly to the army in just the degree that they became friendly to the government. However much they might be divided by antagonistic interests, all joined hands in the willingness to sacrifice for the warlike preparations. Here the radical democrats and the conservative defenders of feudal privileges joined hands. The proletariat, the Socialist, presented the only opposition.

So it was that the government was extraordinarily strengthened during the last decade, and the possibility of its overthrow, of a revolution, appeared to disappear into the infinite.

The fundamental opposition—not to be confused with

the opposition of the "ins" and "outs" of the office holders and seekers—was more and more confined to the proletariat. Many sections, even of the proletariat, lost their revolutionary impulse, after the last political upheaval of 1890.

This upheaval abolished the worst expressions of the political repression of the proletariat in Germany and Austria. Somewhat earlier in France the last remnants of the era of persecution after the uprising of the Commune had disappeared..

To be sure, social reform and labor legislation have not gotten on. These belong rather to the period when industrial capitalism had devolped to the point where its destructive effect upon the public health had become so evident as to imperatively demand redress, where industrial capital did not absolutely and entirely rule in state and society, where the little capitalists, land holders and a portion of the intellectuals still stood in sharp antagonism to it, and where also the opinion prevailed that it was still possible to keep the proletariat, that had just begun to become a power, satisfied with a little labor legislation. This was the condition in England during the '40s of the previous century. The most significant measure of all its labor legislation, the ten-hour day for laboring women, became a law in 1847.

Continental Europe lingered far behind. It was not until 1877 that the Swiss enacted a federal factory law fixing a maximum day of eleven hours for men and women. Austria provided for a similar maximum labor day in 1885. The period of upheavals that followed the overthrow of Bismarck brought a few small advances in Germany and France. In 1891 the new German law on industry came, which fixed a maximum eleven hour work day for women, who had hitherto been entirely unprotected. In 1892 this same provision was introduced into France.

That was all! Since then no progress has been made worth speaking about. After seventeen years we at last obtained a ten-hour work day for women in Germany. The male workers remain, as always, wholly unprotected.

In the field of labor legislation, and also in every field of social reform, complete stagnation reigns.

But the economic improvement which came since the end of the '80s brought to a number of sections of the working class the possibility, thanks to the increasing demand, for labor power, of improving their condition through the "direct action" of the unions without the help of legislation.

This increasing demand was well marked by the decrease in the emigration from the German empire.

The number of emigrants from Germany has been as follows:

1881	220,902
1887	104,787
1891	120,089
1894	40,964
1900	22,309
1907	31,696

This sudden increase in the demand for labor power created a relatively favorable position for a considerable number of sections of the laborers in their opposition to capital. The unions, which, during the first two decades of the new era beginning in 1870, because of the economic depression and the political oppression in Germany, France and Austria, had developed but slowly, now grew rapidly. This was especially true in Germany, where the economic development was most rapid. The English trade unions, the old champions of the working class, were caught up with and, indeed, passed. Considerable improvements in wages, hours of labor and other conditions of employment were obtained.

In Austria, for example, the membership of the unions

grew in the period from 1892 to 1896 from 46,606 to
448,230. During the period from 1893 to 1907 the German unions affiliated with the Central organization increased from 223,530 to 1,865,506. The English trade
unions, on the contrary, during the period from 1892 to
1906 only grew from 1,500,000 to 2,106,283. They added
but 600,000 members to the German 1,600,000.

But it was not alone in rapidity of growth that German
unions exceeded the English ones during this period.
They presented a higher form of the economic movement.
The English unions were purely a national development,
the children of practice alone. The German unions were
founded and led by the Socialists, who were guided by the
fruitful theory of Marxism. Thanks to this fact, the German trade unions were able, from the beginning, to adopt
a much more effective form. In place of the local and
occupational divisions of the English unions they substi-
tuted the great centralized industrial organizations. They
were able thereby largely to avoid jurisdictional disputes,
as well as the guild-like ossification and aristocratic exclu-
siveness of the English unions. Far more than the English, the German unionists feel themselves the representatives of the whole proletariat and not simply of the organized membership of their own trade. The English unionists are but slowly overcoming these difficulties. The
leadership in the international trade union world is falling
more and more to the German unions, thanks to the fact
that from the beginning they have been consciously or un-
consciously more influenced by the Marxian teachings
than their English comrades.

This brilliant development of the German unions made
all the deeper impression upon the great mass of the proletariat in proportion as the course of social reform in
parliament was checked, and the smaller the practical results attained by the working class during this period
through political methods.

The unions, and along with them the co-operatives, appeared to have the mission, without any political disturbance, simply by utilizing the existing legal foundations, of continually raising the working class, of narrowing the field of capital, and of substituting the "constitutional factory" for capitalist absolutism, and through these transitional stages to gradually, without any sudden break or catastrophe, attain to "industrial democracy."

But while the class antagonisms are apparently steadily softening, elements are already appearing that tend once more to sharpen them.

CHAPTER VIII.

THE SHARPENING OF CLASS ANTAGONISMS.

Simultaneously with the labor union organization proceeded another powerful organization, that threatens constantly to bar the way of the first. This organization is the EMPLOYERS' ASSOCIATION.

We have already considered the growth of the corporation. Trade and banking associations have long existed. Since the '70s of the last century these have been seizing power in industry at a constantly increasing rate. We have already referred to the manner in which the centralization of undertakings in a few hands, the road to which was prepared by the advance of the great industry, has received a powerful impetus by the entrance of the corporation. It furthers the expropriation of the small properties that have been invested in shares of stock by the masters of "high finance," who generally know how to navigate the deep waters of modern economic life much better than the little "savers." Indeed, in many cases artificial whirlpools and abysses are stirred up for the express purposes of engulfing these little capitalists. The corporation also brings together the small sums invested in shares into a powerful property completely controlled by the masters of high finance who rule these corporations. The corporation finally makes it possible for great individual financiers, individual millionaires, and great banks, to bring numerous industries under their control much more quickly, and to unite them in a common organization before gaining complete possession.

Thanks to the corporation, we have seen employers' associations shoot up like mushrooms since the '90s. These take on different forms, according to the state of legislation in the various countries. All, however, have the same object—the creation of artificial monopolies by increasing profits. This is sought partially through raising the price of the products, also through increased exploitation of the consumers, and partially through reduction of the cost of production, which is accomplished either through the discharge or increased exploitation of labor or, more frequently, by both.

Still easier than the joining together into combines and trusts for the maintenance of prices, is the formation of organization for the suppression of laborers. In this latter field there is no competition, no antagonism, all are united. It is not only all the employers in any one branch of industry that feel themselves united by a common interest, but the same bonds unite all those in the various branches of industry. However great their enmity as buyers and sellers in the goods market may be, in the labor market they are all united by the most brotherly ties as purchasers of the same commodity—labor power.

These employers' associations offer every possible obstacle to the progress of the working class through labor organizations. Naumann has exaggerated their strength in the extracts quoted above. But the victorious progress of the unions is more restricted during recent years. They are everywhere being placed on the defensive. Ever more frequently and more effectively is the strike met with the lockout. The favorable periods in which successful battles may still be fought are more infrequent.

This situation is made still worse by the ever increasing

flood of needy foreign labor power. This is a natural and necessary result of the industrial growth that has extended the world market with steamships and railroads until the most distant corners of the earth have been opened for the introduction of the products of capitalist industry. In the newly opened localities these products displace those of domestic industry, especially of peasant house industry. This means upon the one side the awakening of new needs in the dwellers in such newly opened localities, and on the other hand it renders necessary the possession of *money*. At the same time the destruction of these home industries renders labor power superabundant in such backward localities. This labor power soon finds itself without any occupation in its old home, and certainly without any money earning occupation. The new means of transportation, steamships and railroads, that have brought them the industrial products of other countries, now offer them the possibility of shipping as living return freight to these industrial countries, where wage earning labor is in sight.

The exchange of men for goods is one of the unavoidable results of the extension of the market for capitalist industry. At first it brings the industrial products of its own country from the city to the open country, and draws back to the city not simply raw material and food products, but labor power also. As soon as an industrial country becomes an exporting country it soon begins to import men. So it was at first in England during the first half of the last century when it drew hordes of workers, especially from Ireland.

To be sure, this flood of backward *(tiefstehender)* elements is a serious obstacle to the proletarian class struggle, but it is naturally and necessarily united with the extension of industrial capitalism. It does not do to do as some "practical politicians" of Socialism wish, and praise this extension of capitalism as a blessing for the proletariat and immigration of foreigners as a curse which has nothing to do with the blessing. Each economic advance is under the system of capitalism united with a curse for the proletariat. If the American laborers wish an influx of Japanese and Chinese, then they must also oppose the carrying of American goods in American steamships to Japan and China, for the purpose of building railroads there with American money. One thing is inseparably connected with the other. '

The immigration of foreigners is a means of keeping the proletariat down, just the same as in the reduction of machines, the substitution of men by women in industry, or of skilled by unskilled workers. Its oppressive results furnish a reason for hostility, not to the foreign workers, but to the domination of capitalists, and for renouncing all illusions that the rapid development of capitalist industry can bring any permanent advantage to the laborers. All such advantages are ever transient.

The bitter end inevitably comes later. Once more this fact becomes evident.

We have already noticed the great reduction in emigration from Germany during the last twenty years. At the same time the number of foreigners in Germany has increased, as is shown by the following figures:

1880	276,057	1900	778,698
1890	433,254	1905	1,007,179

The enumeration always takes place on the first of December when building and agricultural work is at a standstill. The numerous foreign laborers who work in Germany only during the summer, returning to their homes in autumn, are not included in this count.

The difficulties added to the economic battle by the employers' associations and the influx of unattached, unorganized, unprotected strange laborers was rendered doubly bitter by the rise in the price of food products.

One of the most important factors in maintaining the standard of life of the European working class was the fall in the price of food products since the '70s, to which we have already referred. It raised the purchasing power of their money wages, softened the effect of their fall during crises, and during the time of revival permitted the real wages to rise faster than money wages, in so far as agrarian taxes did not offset the favorable effect of lowering food prices.

But within a few years the price of food products has again begun to rise.

This movement can be most clearly followed in England, where it has been unaffected by any agrarian tariff. According to Conrad's table the price of wheat per ton was:

	Mark.		Mark.
1871-75	246.4	1886-90	142.8
1876-80	206.8	1891-95	128.2
1881-85	180.4	1896	123.0

On the other hand, in recent times, according to the quarterly statistics of the German Empire, prices are as follows. In Liverpool La Plata wheat from July to September was:

	Mark.		Mark.
1901	129.1	1905	144.8
1902	.....	1906	138.0
1903	139.3	1907	160.0
1904	152.1	1908	176.0

Naturally the price has varied in the different years with good or bad harvests. But it, nevertheless, appears as if we were now confronted with a rising price of food products, not as a temporary but a permanent phenomenon.

The bankruptcy of Russian agriculture, together with the transformation of the United States from an agricultural to an industrial nation, makes it probable that the gigantic stream of cheap food products which has flowed toward Europe will gradually dry up.

The American wheat production, for example, has not been increasing for several years. It has been as follows:

Year.	Cultivated Area, Acres.	Crop, Bushels.	Av. Price Per Bushel, Dec. 1.
1901	49,900,000	748,000,000	$0.624
1902	46,200,000	670,000,000	.630
1903	49,500,000	633,000,000	.695
1904	44,100,000	552,000,000	.924
1905	48,900,000	693,000,000	.748
1906	47,300,000	735,000,000	.667
1907	45,200,000	634,000,000	.874

It is thus evident that production is rather decreasing than increasing. Consequently the price shows a decided tendency to increase.

The effect of the stoppage in the importation of food products is made worse.by the capitalist combines that artificially raise all prices and freights.

All this is aside from the agrarian tariffs by which the state still further adds to the burden which increasing prices lay upon the laborer.

Added to all this the crisis which came at the end of the year 1907, bringing with it widespread unemployment and the condition of the proletariat became a frightful one, which it remains today. But it is not to be expected that the end of the crisis will bring with it any such upward movement as marked the period from 1895 to 1907. The high price of food products will remain and rise yet higher. The flood of cheap labor power from without will not cease; on the contrary, it will set in with increased power on the appearance of somewhat improved conditions. Most important of all the employers' associations will form an even stronger iron ring, which it will be impossible to break by purely union methods.

However important, and indeed indispensable, the unions have been and will remain, we need not expect that they can again so mightily advance the proletariat by purely economic methods as they were able to do during the last dozen years. We may even need to reckon with the possibility that their opponents will gain sufficient power to gradually force them back.

It is worthy of notice that even during the last years of prosperity, while industry was still in full swing, and was even complaining of a lack of labor power, that the workers were no longer able to raise their real wages—that is, their wages as measured not in money, but in the necessaries of life. This has been proven by private investigations in various sections of the workers in Germany. In America we have an *official recognition* of this fact for the whole laboring class.

The labor bureau at Washington has, since 1890, undertaken each year to investigate the condition of the workers in a number of establishments of the most important branches of industry in the United States. In recent years there were 4,169 factories and work places in which the height of wages, the hours of labor, as well as the domestic budgets of the laborers were investigated, together with the form of their consumption and the prices of the necessaries of life. The figures thus obtained were then compared to show the improvement or deterioration in the condition of the workers.

For each individual article the average of the figures from 1890-99 was taken as 100. The number 101, therefore, indicated an improvement of one per cent as compared with the years 1890-99; the number 99, in the same way, indicated a deterioration of one per cent.

Year—	Weekly Wages of a Workingman Continuously Employed.	Retail Price of Necessaries of Life in Workingman's Budget.	Purchasing Power of Weekly Wages.
1890	101.0	102.4	98.6
1891	100.8	103.8	97.1
1892	100.3	101.9	99.4
1893	101.2	104.4	96.9
1894	97.7	99.7	98.0
1895	98.4	97.8	100.6
1896	99.5	95.5	104.2
1897	99.2	96.3	103.0
1898	99.9	98.7	101.2
1899	101.2	99.5	101.7
1900	104.1	101.1	103.0
1901	105.9	105.2	100.7
1902	109.2	110.9	98.5
1903	112.3	110.3	101.8
1904	112.2	111.7	100.4
1905	114.0	112.4	101.4
1906	118.5	115.7	102.4
1907	122.4	120.6	101.5

First of all this table shows us how much of a basis there is for the so-called "improvement through reform" of the proletariat. The last seventeen years were uncommonly favorable ones for the working class. They were years of such tempestuous upward leaping in America as perhaps may never come again. No working class enjoys greater liberties than the American. None is so "practical" in its politics, freer from all revolutionary theories that might attract its attention from the detail work of improving its condition. Nevertheless, in the year of prosperity, 1907, when the money wage rose an average of 4 per cent above that of the previous year, actual wages were only a trifle higher than in 1890, when business was by no means exceptionally good. To be sure, unemployment and the uncertainty of existence make an enormous difference between a time of prosperity and a crisis; but the purchasing power of the weekly wages of the fully-

employed laborer has changed but a trifle from 1800
to 1907.

Money wages, to be sure, have increased quite largely.
They fell during the period of depression from 1890 to
1894 from 101 to 97.7, or more than 3 per cent, but from
then on they grew steadily, until in 1907 they reached the
figure indicated by 122.4, or almost 25 per cent.

The prices of the *necessaries of life,* on the contrary,
fell more rapidly than wages during the period from 1890
to 1896, the decrease being from 102.4 to 95.5, or about 7
per cent, so that the purchasing power of a week's wages
did not fall as fast as the money income. Actual wages,
in the period from 1890 to 1896, fell only from 98.6 to 98,
or only .6 of one per cent, while money wages had fallen
around 3 per cent. From 1894 to 1896 money wages rose
from 97.7 to 99.5, while the cost of living fell still faster.
So it was that in 1896 the purchasing power of the wages
of an average laborer reached the point indicated by 104.2.

His money wages have never since been able to purchase an equal amount. In spite of all prosperity actual
wages are LOWER NOW THAN TEN YEARS AGO. And this
is what they call a slow but sure *rise* of the laborers!

It is equally worthy of notice that in the very highest
intoxication of business, when the capitalists were grab-
bing their fattest profits, the actual wages of labor did not
even hold their own, but had already began to sink. . To
be sure, the index number indicating money wages increased from 1906 to 1907 from 118.5 to 122.4, almost 4
per cent, but the price of the necessities of life moved
even more swiftly upward from 115.7 to 120.6, or nearly
5 per cent, so that the purchasing power of a week's
wages actually sank one per cent. In reality the relation
was much worse. American statistics are not ordinarily
fixed up so as to make existing conditions blacker than
the facts justify.

All this gives rise to a foreboding that after the passage

of the crisis and the reappearance of prosperity, the proletariat need expect no repetition of the former glorious industrial era.

Let it be repeated that this does not mean that the unions will be powerless or by any means superfluous. They will remain the great mass-organizations of the proletariat without which it would be delivered up helpless to be completely despoiled. The change in the situation does not lessen their importance, but only demands that their methods of fighting be transformed. Where they have to deal with powerful employers' associations they can accomplish little directly, but their battles with such organizations grow to gigantic proportions, and where all concessions are refused by the employers such conflicts may shake all society and the state and influence governments and parliaments.

Strikes in those branches of industry that are dominated by employers' associations, and which play an important part in the general economic life tend more and more to take on a *political* character. On the other hand, opportunities come with increasing frequency in the purely political struggles (for example, battles for the suffrage) in which mass-strikes may be used as an effective weapon.

So it is that the unions are compelled more and more to take up political tasks. In England as in France, in Germany as well as in Austria, they are turning more and more toward politics. This is the justified kernel of the syndicalism of the Romance countries. Unfortunately, however, as a result of its anarchistic origin this kernel is buried in a desert of anti-parliamentarism. And yet this "direct action" of the unions can operate effectively only as an AUXILIARY and RE-ENFORCEMENT TO and not as a SUBSTITUTE FOR parliamentary action.

The center of gravity of the proletarian movement is again resting, even more than during the last two decades, in *politics*. In the first place, proletarian interests are naturally directed toward social reform and protection for labor. In these fields, however, there is almost universal stagnation, which with the present relative forces on the basis of the present governmental foundations cannot be overcome.

By stagnation we do not necessarily understand a complete cessation of movement. That is impossible in such a wildly agitated society as ours. There may be, however, such a slow rate of advance, that it amounts to a complete cessation, or even to a backward movement in comparison with the rate of technical and economic transformation and the increase in exploitation. And this unspeakably slow progress must be secured only through great economic battles, carefully prepared for and fought out. The burdens and sacrifices of such battles tend to rapidly increase and ever more to overbalance the definite results.

It must not be forgotten that our "positive" and "reformatory" work not only strengthens the proletariat, but also arouses our opponents to more energetic resistence to us. The more the battle for social reforms becomes a political battle the more do the employers' associations seek to sharpen the antagonism of parliaments and governments toward the laborers, and to cripple their political powers.

So it is that once more the battle for political rights is being forced into the foreground, and constitutional questions that touch the very foundations of governmental life are becoming live questions.

The opponents of the proletariat are constantly seeking to limit the political rights of the workers. In Germany every electoral victory of the proletariat is followed by threats to substitute a system of plural voting for the present universal suffrage. In France and Switzerland the militia are turned upon the strikers. In England and America it is the courts that are restricting the freedom of

the proletariat, since parliament and congress lack the
courage to openly attack the workers.

But the proletariat cannot be satisfied to simply guard
itself against such attacks. Its condition will be more and
more threatened if it is unable to conquer new positions
in the national life, which will enable it to utilize the governmental institutions in the service of its class interests.
In Germany especially is it in need of this, even more
than any other country save Russia. Already the Reichstag suffrage is being turned more and more against the
city proletariat. The distribution of districts for the
Reichstag elections is today the same as it was in 1871.
But we have seen to what extent the relation of city and
country has changed since then. While in 1871 two-
thirds of the population was in the country and but one-
third in the cities, today that proportion is reversed, while
the relative representation in the Reichstag remains the
same. This more and more favors the open country at
the expense of the city. In the last Reichstag election the
Socialists received 29 per cent of all the votes cast, but
only 10.8 per cent of the representatives. The Center
party, on the contrary, received 19.4 per cent of the votes
and 26.4 per cent of the representatives, and the Conservatives 9.4 per cent of the votes and 15.7 per cent of the
representatives.

These two parties combined did not have as many votes
as the Socialists, but they have four times as many representatives. Under proportional voting the Socialists
would have had 116 instead of 43 representatives in 1907
and the Conservatives and Center together would have
but 115 instead of 164.

The continuation of the present districting is equivalent
to giving a plural vote to the more backward portion of
the population, and this inequality increases from year to
year in the same degree that the city proletariat grows.

Along with this we have a system of casting the votes,

especially in the country and the small cities, that subjects
the proletariat to a political dependence upon the possessing classes in almost as great a degree as their economic
dependence, since the voting envelopes as now used destroy the secrecy of the ballot almost as effectively as the
previous system.

To be sure, the removal of this abuse alone would not
be sufficient. Of what avail is the increase in our influence, and our power in the Reichstag, when the Reichstag
itself is without influence and power? Power must first
be conquered for it. A genuine parliamentary regime
must be established. The imperial government must be a
committee of the Reichstag.

The Reichstag is weakened, not alone because the imperial government is independent of it, but no less from
the fact that the empire is by no means a complete united
state. Its power is further restricted by the sovereignty
of the separate states, by their governments and landtags,
and their narrow particularism. It would be easy enough
to deal with the smaller states, did not one mighty mass
lay athwart the way—PRUSSIA and her Langtag, elected
by the three-class system of voting. The particularism of
Prussia, above all, must be broken, her Landtag must
cease to be the shield of all reaction. The conquest of
secret and equal suffrage for the North German Landtags,
and above all for that of Prussia, and the raising of the
Reichstag to the position of dominant power, are the most
imperative political tasks of the day.

But even if we were able in this manner to transform
Germany into a democratic state, that would not be
enough to help the proletariat forward. The German
proletariat, that already constitutes a majority of the
population, would, to be sure, have the key to legislation
in its hand. But this would do it very little good if the
state did not possess the rich resources that are indispensable to social reform.

Today, however, all the resources of the state are eaten up by the *military* and *naval* expenditures. The steady growth of these expenditures is responsible for the fact that the present state neglects even those cultural undertakings that are of the most imperative interest for the whole population, and not of the proletariat alone, such as the improvement of education, and of means of communication—canals and roads, etc.—undertakings that would greatly increase the productive and competitive power of the country, and are accordingly demanded by the purely business interests of capitalism.

But no large sums can be secured for these purposes, since the army and the navy devour everything, and will always continue to devour everything so long as the present system rules.

The *abolition of the standing army and disarmament* is indispensable if the state is to carry out any important reforms. Even capitalist elements are coming more and more to recognize this, but they are incapable of accomplishing it. Peace prattle by philanthropists will not take us a single step forward.

The present competitive preparation for war is primarily a result of the colonial policy and imperialism, and so long as this policy is maintained it will do little good to preach peace. The colonial policy involves militarism, and it is foolish to set a definite aim and then try to avoid the means by which it can be attained. This ought to suggest something to some of our friends, who are shouting for world peace and disarmament, attending all the bourgeois peace congresses, and at the same time advocating the colonial policy, although, to be sure, they always advocate an ethical, socialist colonial policy. They are in the same position as those Prussian liberals of the '70s of the last century, who as capitalist politicians feared the revolution, and who sought to secure the unity of Germany, not through a revolution, but by the triumph of the

house of Hohenzollern, and at the same time as democratic politicians sought to restrict militarism and refused
to grant the Hohenzollerns the miltary force with which
to perform their task.   They were destroyed by their own
contradictions.

Whoever stands for the colonial policy must also stand
for competitive armament.   Whoever would check this
must convince the people of the useless and indeed of the
ruinousness of the colonial policy.

In the present situation that is the most imperative political task of the militant proletariat; that is the "positive"
policy that it must follow.   Until this problem is solved
there is little hope of securing any "reforms" of any importance in the face of the growth of employers' associations, of the rise in the cost of living, of the flood of low
standard workers, of the universal stagnation in all legislative social reform, of the growth of the national expenses under this burden.

The improvement of the right of suffrage for the Reichstag, the conquest of equal and secret ballot for the Landtags, especially of Saxony and Prussia, the gaining of a
dominant position for the Reichstag not only over the imperial government, but also over the individual states,
these are the special tasks of the German proletariat. The
battle against imperialism and militarism is the common
task of the whole international proletariat.

Many may think that the accomplishment of these tasks
would not bring any great advance.   Does not Switzerland offer an example of a state that fulfills all these
conditions—complete democracy, popular militia system,
and no colonial policy?   Yet social reform stagnates in
Switzerland and the proletariat is exploited and enslaved
by the employers just as everywhere else.

On this point the first thing to note is that the Swiss
do not escape the consequences of the competitive armament that is going on around them, but, on the contrary,

are industriously entering upon the same competition and
spending no small amounts thereby. A portion of the
military expenses are borne by the various cantons, but
in spite of this the expenditures of the central government are growing by leaps and bounds, as is shown by
the following table:

Year—	Francs.	Year—	Francs,
1875	39,000,000	1905	117,000,000
1885	41,000,000	1906	129,000,000
1895	79,000,000	1907	139,000,000

The appropriations for the military are growing rapidly,
as is also the income from taxes. They are as follows:

Year—	Appropriations for Militarism	Receipts of Finance and Tax Departments
1895	23,000,000	4,000,000
1905	31,000,000	64,000,000
1906	35,000,000	62,000,000
1907	42,000,000	63,000,000

If we omit the income and expenditures for the postal
and telegraph systems, that nearly cancel each other, we
find that in 1907 the income was eighty-three million
francs, of which seventy-three million were raised from
taxation. The expenses amounted to eighty million
francs, of which forty-two million were for the military
and six million for interest on the public debt.

So we see that even in Switzerland militarism is swal-
lowing up the lion's share of the national income, and
that its demands are rapidly growing.

No one would be so naive as to assert that we can pass
unperceptibly and without a battle from the military
state and absolutism into democracy, and out of the con-
quering imperialism into the union of free peoples by a
gradual "growing into." The whole idea of "growing
into" can only arise during a time when it is the common
belief that all further evolution will take place exclusively
on the economic field, without any change whatever being
required in the relation of political powers and institu-

tions. As soon as it becomes evident that such changes
are imperatively necessary for the proletariat if its economic elevation is to proceed further, this compels the
recognition of the necessity of political struggles, trans-
fers of power and transformations.

The proletariat must grow mightily in these struggles.
It cannot win these battles, cannot reach the above men-
tioned goals of democracy and abolition of militarism,
without itself attaining to a dominant position in the state.
So it is that the acquisition of democracy and the abolition
of militarism in a modern great nation have wholly different results, than rise at the present time from the old
inherited militia system and the republican institutions of
the Swiss.

This is all the more true in proportion as these transformations are accomplished exclusively by the proletariat. And there is no prospect of any faithful allies in
the coming battles. Hitherto we have reckoned upon
allies from the capitalist camp, namely, small capitalists
and small farmers.

We have seen how earnestly Marx and Engels for a
long time expected that the small capitalist democracy
would at least start a revolution with us as they had done
in 1848 and 1871. As the democratic policies and parties
continued more and more to prove disappointing, we
Marxians still continued to believe that great masses of
the little capitalists and small farmers would be drawn
to us, and interested in our revolutionary objects. In my
articles of 1893 which have already been quoted, these
expectations found even stronger expression than in
Engels' introduction written in 1895:

> "If this continues, by the end of the century we
> will have captured the larger portion of the middle
> classes of society, small capitalists and small farmers,
> and will have grown to be a deciding power in the
> country."

These expectations have not been fulfilled.   But we have here another illustration of how we Marxists, with our expectations and our "prophecies," were wrong when we overvalued the revolutionary sentiments of the small capitalists.   We also see how much foundation there is for the reproach that Marxian dogmatic fanaticism drove these elements out of the party.   When Engels in 1894 opposed the French farmers' program, and when I opposed the German one a year later, this was not because we considered the gaining of the farmers as superfluous, but because we considered these methods the wrong ones with which to win them.   Since then the party membership in France, Austria, and Switzerland has tried their fortune among the farmers along these lines without success.

The same is true of the small capitalists.   It must be granted that so far as large sections of the middle class are concerned, and whatever forms of propaganda have been used, that they are today more difficult to win than ever before.

This conclusion is not based on Marxian "orthodoxy" —we have already seen that Marxism has erred rather by expecting too much than too little at this point—it is the result of bitter experience during recent years.

Our Marxian "dogmatic fanaticism" therefore is not concerned in the matter, except in so far as it makes it easier for us to recognize and understand these experiences, and to lay bare their causes—the indispensable condition to any real "practical politics."

Here again we find that our "positive" work, as soon as it strengthens the proletariat, by just that very fact, sharpens the antagonism between it and other classes.

Many of us expected that the trusts and combines of the capitalists, together with the tariff policy, would lead the middle class, who suffer most from these things, into our ranks.   The exact reverse has actually been the result.

The agrarian tariff and the employers' associations came simultaneously with the trade unions. So it was that the handicraftsmen were simultaneously pressed from all sides. The tariff and the employers' associations raised the price of the necessities of life and raw material, while the unions raised wages.

To be sure, it was only the money wages and not the real wages that were raised, since prices went up faster than wages. Nevertheless the wage struggle embittered the little bosses, and they came to look upon the employers' associations and the tariff parties as their allies against the organized workers. The latter and not the tariff and trusts were blamed not only for the high money wages, but also for the rise in prices of raw material and rents, which it was claimed were due to the rise of wages.

The little merchants, again, saw themselves squeezed by the rise in prices since the purchasing power of their customers, mostly laborers, did not increase in the same degree. They turned their anger against the laborers rather than against the tariff and the combines. They did this all the more willingly, the more the laborers sought to escape the effect of the rise in prices by trying to abolish the middle men through co-operatives.

It must not be forgotten that the laborer plays a peculiar role in the market for goods. Everyone else comes to this market, not only as buyer, but also as a seller of products. What the trader loses as buyer of goods in the universal rise of prices he gains by the rise of his own products. Only the laborer comes to the world market as a buyer alone and not as a seller of goods. His labor power is a peculiar sort of goods, with peculiar price laws, so that wages do not automatically follow general changes in price. Labor power is not something apart from men, but is inseparable from and closely bound up with the lives of human beings. Beneath its price are psychological, physiological and historical conditions, that do not affect other wares and which introduce an element of permanence into money wages greater than exists in regard to other goods.

Wages follow price movements, but slowly and only to a certain degree. The possessor of labor power gains more in declines of·price and loses more with rising prices than buyers of other products. His standpoint in the goods market is in antagonism to that of the sellers. In spite of the fact that he produces all and consumes but a portion of his product, his standpoint is that of the consumer and not that of the producer. His product does not belong to him, but to his exploiters, the capitalists.

It is the capitalist who appears upon the market as a producer and seller with the product of the labor of the wage worker. The laborer appears there only as the buyer of the means of life.

In consequence of these facts the laborers are placed in antagonism to the sellers and also to the farmers in so far as they are sellers. It is not alone on the question of the tariff on agricultural products, but on many other points, for example, the attempt to raise the price of milk, that the farmers and the laborers stand in sharp antagonism.

The farmers, in so far as they employ wage workers, are embittered by the attempts to raise wages and improve the conditions of the industrial workers. The time of industrial prosperity and the strengthening of the unions and their victories was also the time of insufficient labor in agriculture. Not only the hired men and the hired girls, but even the children of the farmers, were drawn away to industry in ever increasing swarms, seeking to escape the barbaric conditions of life in agriculture. Naturally the accursed Socialists were blamed for this lack of labor power in the country.

So it has happened that increasing sections of those classes of the population that formerly constituted the nucleus of the little capitalist democracy, and energetic fighters in its revolution, and who had been at least somewhat indifferent allies of the revolutionary proletariat, now turned everywhere into its most violent enemies. This was still least true in "Marxian soaked" Germany, and much more in France, Germany and Switzerland.

In the great cities the enmity of the middle classes to the proletariat was increased still more by their antagonistic positions on the questions of imperialism and colonial policy. Whoever rejects the Socialist position has nothing left but despair unless he believes in the colonial policy. It is the only prospect before the defenders of capitalism. But along with it must go the acceptance of militarism and the big navy. Even those sections of the middle class that are not in the direct circle of interest of hand work, retail trade, or the production of necessaries of life, such as the intellectuals are also, in so far as they are not permeated with Socialism, being driven away from the proletariat and its far-seeing vision, by being thrown into the current of imperialism and militarism. All those who, like Barth, Brentano, and Naumann, once looked so favorably upon the trade union and co-operative organization of the proletariat and its democratic efforts, are today defenders of big fleets and expansion. Their friendship for the Socialists lasts only so long as imperialism and its consequences are not concerned.

These policies seem destined to complete the isolation of the proletariat and thereby doom it to political barrenness at the very moment when its political development is needed more than ever.

Yet it is possible that this very policy of imperialism may become the starting point for the overthrow of the present ruling system.

CHAPTER IX.

We have seen how rapidly the cost of militarism has risen in Switzerland. That, however, is little more than a weak reflection of what is taking place in the great military nations. Let us now turn to the German empire. According to the statistical year book of the German empire the following have been the expenditures for this purpose, in millions of marks:

	1873	1880-81	1891-92	1900	1908
Army	308	370	488	666	856
Navy	26	40	85	152	350
Colonial government	..	..	..	21	21
Pensions	21	18	41	68	110
Interest on public debt	..	9	54	78	156
Totals	355	437	668	985	1493
Annual increase		12	21	35	64
				2056	
Total government expense	404	550	1118	*1640	2785
Annual increase		21	52	58	91

We see that the expenses rise steadily, but in an ever increasing rate. During the first decade of the empire the increase was in the neighborhood of 21,000,000 a year. Finally during the last decade the increase rose at the rate of nearly 91,000,000 a year, and during these last years the yearly increase reached almost 200,000,000.

The principal increase is in the cost of the preparations

*From 1900 on the expense of postoffice, railroads and government printing are included. These amounted in 1900 to 416,000,-000 marks.

for war. Of these the cost of the navy rises more rapidly
than that of the army. While the population of the empire during the years from 1891 to 1908 increased from
50,000,000 to 60,000,000, or about ONE-FOURTH, the cost
of the army has in the meantime almost DOUBLED, the expenditures for pensions and interest on the public debt
have TRIPLED, and the naval expenses have QUADRUPLED.
And there can be no halt in this mad increase until the
present system is changed from the VERY FOUNDATION.
The continuous technical transformation which is bringing the capitalist machine system and natural science into
the field of production forces its way into the art of war,
and there creates a continuous competition of new dis-
coveries, a continuous depreciation of what now exists,
and a continuous extension of power, but not, as in the
field of production, a continuous increase in the produc-
tivity of labor, but a continuous aggravation of the de-
structiveness of war and a continuous increase in the un-
productive wastes of peace.

Along with the transformation through technical evolution there goes also a constant extension of the domination, or at least of the sphere of influence of every great
nation, due to the policy of expansion, which in turn
makes necessary ever increasing armament.

So long as the policy of expansion continues the delusion of competitive armament must continue to increase
until complete exhaustion is reached. Imperialism, however, as we have already seen, is the single hope, the single
idea of the future which offers anything to present society.
Consequently this delusion will increase until the proletariat gains the power to determine the policy of the nation,
to overthrow the policy of imperialism and substitute the
policy of Socialism. The longer this competitive armament continues, the heavier the load that will be laid upon
the people of each country. Consequently each class will
seek more and more to shove these loads off upon other

classes, and therefore the more this competitive armament will tend to sharpen class antagonism.

In Germany it is naturally the laborers upon whom the heaviest load is shoved. This was bad enough in a time of industrial prosperity, of low cost of living, of advancing trade unions. It becomes unbearable in a time of crisis, of rising prices, of the ascendancy of employers' associations. But the increasing load of taxes does not simply diminish the income of the laborers and reduce the purchasing power of their wages. It greatly threatens industrial progress itself, which the policy of expansion pretends to further.

The United States is the most dangerous competitor of German industry. The latter is greatly handicapped in this struggle by the German tariff system. To be sure, America has an even higher tariff. But it is an INDUSTRIAL and not an AGRARIAN tariff. It is provided with the cheapest food products and produces nearly all raw materials itself. Along with this it possesses the advantage of having no important land power as neighbor. It does not need to draw more than half a million men year in and year out from production to engage in the foolish waste of soldiery.

The more militarism grows in Europe, the greater grows the industrial superiority of the United States, and the more the economic progress of Europe languishes. Consequently, the more unfavorable grows the economic condition of the European working class. And in order to further this process the greatest sacrifices are demanded of us.

To be sure, the United States has also entered upon the road of imperialism and therewith upon the road of increased military preparations. Since the war with Spain the expenses for army and navy have been increasing. Nevertheless they are still less injured by this than the great powers of Europe, since, unlike these, they do not need to maintain a great standing army at home. In the whole United States there are barely 60,000 men in the army.*

As in the field of industrial competition, the United States can still go a long ways in military competition before it is exhausted.

The following table shows the position of the United States in these respects in round millions:

| | Population | National Debt | Expense of Army | Expense of Navy | Value of Exports Per Cent of Total | | |
					Food Prod.	Raw Material	Manufacturing
1880....	50	1919	38	14	56	29	15
1890....	63	890	45	22	42	36	21
1900....	76	1101	135	56	40	24	35
1907....	86	879	123	97	28	32	40

We see that the national debt of the United States is decreasing. To be sure, it increased in 1900, together with the expenditures for the army, as a result of the war with Spain. But since then it has again decreased in spite of increasing expenditures for the army and navy. The cost of the land forces for 1908 was $190,000,000, almost as much as in Germany, although, to be sure, with a population of eighty-six million.

The table of exports, however, shows how rapidly the export of manufactured articles from America is increasing and how much it is growing to be an industrial and not an agricultural nation in relation to the world market.

Out of a total export of $1,875,000,000 worth of goods from Germany in 1907, $1,750,000,000 were manufactured goods. In the United States, out of a total export of $1,853,000,000 worth of goods of domestic production, over $740,000,000 worth were manufactured articles. In 1890 the value of the manufactured goods exported from

---

*This, of course, does not include the militia.—Trans.

Germany amounted to $530,000,000 and of the United States to $170,000,000. Since then Germany has increased its exports of manufactures 150 per cent and the United States 300 per cent.

It is evident that the United States is already pushing Germany hard as an industrial nation.

And in this situation, while the United States in the period from 1900 to 1907 reduced its national debt in the neighborhood of $230,000,000, Germany increased its load of debt during the same period about $360,000,000. And even now, while this is being written, new colossal increases in expenses and higher taxation to raise a half million more are being planned.

The working class are struck hardest by these loads and crushed down, and this hampers industry, and handicaps the nation in its competitive struggle, which again reacts upon the laborers, upon whose shoulders this whole battle is fought. But there is a limit to the burden the laborers can bear, so at last this competitive armament cripples industrial progress.

At the same time the national antagonisms grow sharper, which stirs up the danger of war. Each government finds the constant and ever revolutionized war preparations more unbearable, but none of the ruling classes seeks the fault in the world politics that they follow. They dare not see it there, for this is the last refuge of capitalism. So each one finds the fault with the other, the German with England and the English with Germany. All become more and more nervous and suspicious, which in turn creates a new spur, to add new haste to the warlike preparations, until they are at last ready to cry: "Better a terrible end than an endless terror."

Long ago this situation would have led to war, as the only alternative except revolution by which to escape from this crazy situation of reciprocal screwing up of the national burdens, had it not been for the fact that this alternative would have brought the revolution that stands behind the war—nearer than even behind an armed peace. It is the rising power of the proletariat which for three decades has prevented every European war, and which today causes every government to shudder at the prospect of war. But forces are driving us on to a condition where at last the weapons will be automatically released.

There is another phenomenon that is working in the same direction, and which, even more than the competitive arming, is destined to reduce the policy of expansion to an *ad absurdum,* and thereby to cut off from the present method of production its last possibility of further evolution.

The policy of expansion or imperialism rests upon the supposition that only peoples belonging to the European civilization are capable of independent development. The people of other races are looked upon as children, idiots, or beasts of burden who may be handled with more or less gentleness, and in any case are beings of a lower stage, which can be controlled according to our desires. Even Socialists have proceeded upon this supposition so far as to advocate colonization—to be sure, in an ethical manner. But actual events soon teach them that the fundamental principle of our party—the equality of all men—is not a mere phrase, but a very real power.

To be sure, the peoples who are outside the circle of influence of European civilization are almost incapable of any resistance during this century. This does not rest upon any natural inferiority, as the conceited ignorance of European bourgeois scholars would have us believe, whose science finds expression in the phantasies of our racial theoreticians. These people are crushed simply by the superiority of European technical development, including, to be sure, European mentality, which, in the last analysis, rests upon that technical development.

With the exception of some very backward branches

including but a few thousand men, the peoples belonging to non-European civilizations are fully capable of taking up that civilization, but the material conditions hitherto have been lacking.

The extension of capitalism changes these conditions but little. Capitalist exportation brings into the localities lying outside the scope of European civilization (within which America and Australia are, of course, included) at first only capitalist PRODUCTS, and not capitalist PRODUCTION. Most important of all, even this influence is confined to the waterways, the sea coast and a few great rivers.

A tremendous transformation has taken place in this respect during the last generation, and especially during the last two decades. They have not only brought a new era of transoceanic conquest. The exports from industrial countries to undeveloped lands are no longer composed exclusively of PRODUCTS; they now include the INSTRUMENTS OF PRODUCTION AND TRANSPORTATION of modern industrialism.

We have already seen what a rapid advance there has been in railroad construction during recent years, especially in the Orient (Russia is here included). But capitalist industry is also rapidly developing in these countries. This is especially true of the textile and iron industries and mining. The latter has revolutionized South Africa.

It is from this export of the means of production that capitalist industry has drawn its new blood since the second half of the '80s of the last century. It appeared to be at the end of its capacity for expansion by the first half of the '80s, and it really was, so far as the export of manufacture is concerned. But the export of the means of production made possible a wholly unexpected and striking expansion, and developed the capitalist method of production in non-European civilizations, driving the previous economic conditions quickly out of existence. This, however, made impossible the continuance of the old methods of thought in the Orient. Along with the new methods of production of European origin, hitherto barbaric peoples suddenly acquired the intellectual capacity of developing to the European level. This new spirit breathes no love for Europe. The new countries become competitors of the old. But competitors are ENEMIES. The existence of the European spirit in Oriental countries does not make them our friends, but only our equals as enemies. That does not take place immediately. We have already seen what a role the CONSCIOUSNESS OF STRENGTH plays in the social life, and how long a newly rising class or nation may remain in a subservient position which already possesses the power of securing independence, but is not yet conscious of that fact. This is showing itself now. The people of the Orient have been so often conquered by Europeans that they look upon all resistance as hopeless. Europeans have the same opinion. Their colonial policy is based on this, and so they treat, dispose of and deceive these people as if they were cattle.

But as soon as the Japanese broke the ice there was an instant reaction throughout the entire Orient. All Eastern Asia, as well as the whole Mohammedan world, raised to an independent policy, to a resistance against all domination from without.

This brought imperialism to a sudden stop. It can move no further. Yet it must constantly proceed further, since capitalism must constantly expand if its exploitation is not to become absolutely unbearable.

Equatorial Africa remains as the only possible field of expansion, where the climate is the best ally of the native, where European soldiers cannot be used, and where the Europeans must obtain natives as soldiers, and arm and train them—in preparation for the time when these mercenary troops will turn against their masters.

Everywhere in Asia and Africa the spirit of rebellion is spreading, and with it is spreading also the use of European arms, and a growing resistance to European exploitation. It is impossible to transplant capitalist exploitation into any country without therewith sowing the seeds of revolt against that exploitation. This expresses itself first in a growing difficulty in colonial politics, and a constant increase in their cost. Our colonial enthusiasts comfort us for the burdens that the colonies now impose upon us with promises of the rich rewards that the future is to bring. In reality the military expenses for the maintenance of colonies will, from now on, constantly increase—and this will not be all. The majority of the countries in Asia and Africa are reaching a condition in which the temporary uprisings will become open and continuous, and will end with the destruction of the foreign yoke. The British colonies of East India are nearest to this stage; their loss is equivalent to the bankruptcy of the English government.

We have already called attention to the fact that the Russo-Japanese war has inspired Eastern Asia and the Mohammedan world to throw off European capitalism. In this they are fighting the same enemy that the European proletariat is fighting. To be sure, we must not forget that while they are fighting the same enemy they are not fighting it with the same object—not in order to gain a victory for the proletariat over capital, but in order to substitue an internal national capitalism for an external one they are rising. We must not have any illusions on this point. Just as the Boers were the closest skinners of the people, so the Japanese rulers are the worst persecutors of Socialists and the Young Turks have already felt themselves compelled to proceed against striking workers. We must not take an uncritical attitude to the non-European opponents of European capitalism.

This, however, does not alter the fact that these oppo-

nents weaken European capitalism and its governments
and introduce an element of political unrest into the entire
world.

We have seen how in Europe a period of constant political unrest continued from 1789 to 1871, until the industrial bourgeoisie had conquered everywhere the political
positions which their rapid development made possible.
Since the Russo-Japanese war, since 1905, a similar
period of constant political unrest has existed in the
Orient. The people of Eastern Asia and the Mohammedan world, together with those of Russia, have just
entered upon a position in many ways similar to that of
the West European bourgeoisie at the end of the eighteenth and the beginning of the nineteenth century. Naturally the conditions are not wholly the same. One thing
that makes them different is that the world is a hundred
years older. The political development of a country does
not depend entirely upon its own social conditions, but
upon the conditions of the whole surrounding world,
which affect that country. The different classes of Russia,
Japan, India, China, Turkey, Egypt, etc., may stand in a
similar relation to one another as did the classes of France
before the great Revolution. But they will be influenced
by the experiences of the class struggles that have taken
place since then in England, France, and Germany. On
the other hand, their struggle for favorable conditions
for a national capitalist system of production, is at the
same time a struggle against foreign capital and its
foreign domination—a struggle which the people of Western Europe did not have to conduct during their revolutionary period from 1789-1871.

But however great these differences which tend to prevent the East from simply repeating the events of the
West of a century ago, the similarity is still great enough
to make it certain that the East is now entering upon a
revolutionary period of a similar character—a period of

conspiracies, coup d'etats, insurrections; reactions and re-
newed insurrections and continuous transformations that
will continue until the conditions of a peaceful development and a secured national independence is obtained for
this portion of the world.

Thanks to world politics, however, the Orient (using
this word in the widest sense) is so closely connected with
the Occident that the political unrest of the East cannot
but affect the West. The political equilibrium of nations
that has been so carefully obtained is now confronted with
wholly unexpected alterations, that stagger it, and upon
which it can exercise no influence. Problems whose
peaceful solution appears impossible, and that have consequently been avoided and put aside (such, for example,
as the relations of the Balkan states) now suddenly arise
and demand a solution. Unrest, mistrust, uncertainty
everywhere, are forced to a climax through the nervous-
ness already raised to a high degree by the competitive
armament. A world war is brought within threatening
proximity.

The experience of the last decade, however, shows that
war means revolution, that it has as a result great changes
in political power. In 1891 Engels still held that it
would be a great misfortune for us if a war broke out
which should bring a revolution with it, precipitating us
prematurely into power. For some time, he thought, the
proletariat could proceed more securely by the utilization
of the present governmental foundations than by running
the risk of a revolution precipitated by a war.

Since then the situation has changed much. The proletariat has now grown so strong that it can contemplate
a war with more confidence. We can no longer speak of
a PREMATURE revolution, for it has already drawn so great
strength from the present legal basis as to expect that a
transformation of this basis would create the conditions
for its further upward progress.

The proletariat. hates war with all its strength. It would sacrifice everything rather than raise a cry for war. But if war should break out in spite of it, the proletariat is the only class that could confidently await its outcome.

Since 1891 it has not only grown greatly in numbers, not only been solidified by organization, it has also gained enormously in MORAL CONVICTION. Two decades ago the Socialists of Germany were still confronted with the great prestige which the rulers of the empire had gained in the struggles for its foundation. Today that prestige is scattered to the winds.

On the other hand, the more the idea of imperialism becomes bankrupt, the more the Socialists become the only party that is fighting for a great ideal and a great object, that is capable of arousing all the energy and devotion that flows to such an object.

In the ranks of our opponents, on the contrary, hesitation and apathy is sown by the consciousness that incapacity and corruption has degraded their leaders. They no longer believe in their cause, nor in their leaders, who right now, in the face of the situation whose difficulties are increasing from day to day, must fail and continue to fail and to more and more expose their complete incapacity.

This also is no accident, no fault of any individual persons, but is a necessary consequence of conditions.

The causes of this condition are manifold in character. As soon as a class or a government passes out of the revolutionary into the conservative stage, as soon as it is no longer compelled to fight for its existence or its further progress, as soon as it is contented with the present, the intellectual horizon of its spokesmen and rulers is narrowed and confined. Its interest in great questions dies out, it loses the power to do and dare, bold thinkers and fighters become undesirable and are pushed aside.

Petty intrigue and cowardly unprincipleness push to the front.

In the same way the fact that statesmen and thinkers of a class or a country no longer struggle for anything great tends to develop selfish interests, and to cause the interests of individual persons to be pressed forward instead of the general interests of a class, a community or a society. The persons who are striving for power are no longer inspired by the impulse to create something great and new for the community, but only to obtain riches and power for themselves. This unscrupulous striving finds its expression in the efforts of the seekers after power, to attract, not those forces that are most capable of serving the community, but of such as can be most easily utilized to satisfy the needs and inclinations of the seekers for power.

To these general causes of the moral and intellectual collapse of all possessors of power in a conservative stage, must be added certain ones that spring peculiarly from capitalism.

Hitherto the exploiting classes have been the governing classes. They at least reserved the apexes of the governing machinery for themselves. The capitalist class, on the contrary, is so filled with the greed for business profits, that it relinquishes politics to others, who, to be sure, are at bottom but its agents. In democratic countries they are professional politicians, parliamentarians and journalists, in absolutisms the court circle, in intermediate nations, a mixture of these two elements with sometimes one, sometimes the other dominating.

So long as capitalist exploitation is small, the watchword of capital is economy, and it seeks to introduce this into the administration of government also. The small capitalists are forced, willy-nilly, to remain true to this watchword. The big capitalists, on the contrary, as the degree of exploitation rises practice ostentation and extravagance, that finally reaches such a mad pace as finds its extreme in insane forms of competitive armament.

In other ages the rulers of the state led all their subjects in display. Now the politicians and the statesmen even in the highest places are left far behind by the kings of high finance. It is difficult to increase the income of the government officials from the national treasury, especially in paliamentary nations, where heed must be paid to the voters and taxpayers who are always crying for economy. This is all the more difficult as the preparations for war absorb all the increase in national income.

If the politicians and statesmen are to keep up with the rising standard of living of the great exploiters, there is nothing left for them but to open up illegitimate sources of income alongside of their legitimate ones, by the utilization and prostitution of their political influence. They use their knowledge of governmental secrets and their influence upon governmental policies in speculation on the board of trade; they sponge upon the hospitality of great exploiters in a parasitic manner; they permit such persons to pay their debts, and in the worst cases accept bribes for the sale of their political influence.

The evil of corruption is invariably found wherever there are capitalist states with great exploiters. It always seizes the politically influential organs first, in democratic states the parliamentarians and journalists, in absolutisms the court nobility. Everywhere it breeds a far-reaching corruption that spreads the more rapidly in proportion as the exploitation and extravagance, and therewith the needs of the politicians and officials grow, and the power and the economic functions of the government increase.

To be sure, it is not claimed that all those who are touched by corruption are aware of it, or that all politicians and statesmen of the ruling class are corrupt. That would be to exaggerate. But the TEMPTATION to corruption continuously increases in these circles. It demands a constantly increasing strength of character to resist this temptation. It becomes easier to yield to this temptation the more extensive the atmosphere of corruption and the more developed and insinuating its methods, which do not permit those who are seized by corruption to become conscious of their own downfall.

So we see that in the same degree that the problems of politics become more and more complicated and make greater demands on the knowledge, intellectual activity, foresight and decision of statesmen, that in just the same degree the ruling class substitutes superficial babbling for scientific earnestness, fickleness for intellectual stability, personal rivalry and narrow intrigues in place of calculated pursuit of a distant goal, constant wavering between provocative brutality and cowardly retreat in place of quiet, decisive firmness.

At the same time an almost universal greediness and corruption appears. This manifests itself, now in a Panama scandal, then in an alliance between officials and swindlers, almost everywhere in fraudulent contracts for war material, sometimes in blow-hole armorplate, and again in useless weapons, and in other places again the fatherland is charged double what the same goods are sold for to other countries. For a long time contracts for war material have been a means of enriching the capitalists. Never, however, have the contractors for military supplies been so close to the government as now, never have they had so much influence over the policies that make for peace or war.

These same contractors are today the greatest industrial capitalists, the greatest exploiters of the proletariat. They have the greatest interest in the brutal war upon the inner as well as the outer enemy, and the greatest influence upon the government, which is more and more made up of unstable individuals.

Consequently every state must regard its neighbors, and the working class of every state must look upon its rulers as liable upon the slightest provocation, or as a result of any accident, to release the most inconceivable horrors upon it. All this is bound to produce a new transformation in the little capitalist class.

Naturally the moral bankruptcy of the ruling class is most complete in those localities where it is inaccessible to the mass of the people. Some great catastrophe, like the Russo-Japanese war, is required to expose the full rottenness of the system. In ordinary times it is only here and there that some special unskillfulness lifts a corner of the blanket that at other times shamefully conceals all. The class-conscious proletariat are touched but little by such disclosures. The laborers are much more antagonistic to the ruling class than formerly and do not deceive themselves about its moral qualities.

It is different with the small capitalist class. The more it becomes untrue to its democratic past, the more it crawls under the government and expects help from it, and the more it trusts in that government and its stability, and all the greater its horror when the foundation is torn away and its prestige goes to the devil.

There is a simultaneous increase in the pressure by the great capitalist combines and through the demands of the state upon their purses. This does not improve their confidence in the ruling class.

That confidence must completely disappear when the incapacity, indiscretion and corruption of the governing class frivolously precipitates a catastrophe—a war or a coup d'etat—that would expose the country to extreme distress. The blind rage of the little capitalists would be all the more easily and fiercely turned against the class that chanced to be ruling at such a time in proportion as it had expected much from this class previously, and the more it had exaggerated the ability and honesty of such a ruling class.

The last decade has certainly increased the hatred of the small capitalists for the proletariat. The latter must henceforth direct its policy with the expectation of fighting the coming battle unaided. But Marx has already shown that the little capitalist, as an intermediate thing between the capitalist and proletarian, wavers back and forth between the two, now the man of one and now of the other. We dare not reckon upon him, he will always be an uncertain ally—as a body. Individuals may well become very excellent party comrades, or their enmity to us may grow still greater. But that does not necessarily mean that some day, because of an unbearable burden of taxation and sudden moral collapse of the ruling class, they will come into our ranks en masse and perhaps thereby sweep away our enemies and decide our victory. Certainly it could make no cleverer stroke, for the victorious proletariat offers to all those who are exploiters, to all oppressed and exploited, as well as to all who vegetate like the small capitalists and small farmers, a tremendous betterment in their conditions of life.

However hostile the little capitalist class may be to us today, it is far from being a firm support of the possessing class. It also is wabbling and cracking in all its joints, like every other support of present society.

The security of the existing order is failing in the consciousness of the people as well as in reality. There is a general feeling that we are entering upon a period of general uncertainty, that things cannot go on as they have gone for a generation, that the present situation is becoming rapidly untenable and cannot survive another generation.

In this time of universal uncertainty the immediate task of the proletariat is clear. We have already developed it. It cannot progress further without changes in the national foundation upon which it is waging its fight. To strive for democracy, not only in the empire, but also in the individual states and especially in Prussia—that is its next task in Germany; its next international task is to wage war on world politics and militarism.

Just as clear as these tasks are the means which are at our disposal for their solution. In addition to those that have already been utilized we have now added the MASS-STRIKE, which we had already theoretically accepted at the beginning of the '90s, and whose application under favorable conditions has been repeatedly tested since then. If it has been somewhat pushed into the background since the glorious days of 1905, this only shows that it is not workable in every situation, and that it would be foolish to attempt to apply it under all conditions.

So far the situation is clear. But it is not the proletariat alone that must be considered in the fight that lies before us. Many other factors will participate therein that are wholly incalculable.

Incalculable are our statesmen. Their personalities change rapidly and their views more rapidly still. They no longer have any logical, definite policy.

Incalculable also are the small capitalist masses that, now here, now there, throw their weight into the scale, balancing it up and down.

Furthermore, the insanity of foreign politics, which involves so many nations, is still incalculable, so that the incalculableness of the internal politics of such states is increased manifold by the complications of its foreign relations.

All these factors are now in the closest and most continuous interrelation, so that it is impossible to come to any conclusions concerning them.

The Socialists will be able to assert themselves in the midst of this universal uncertainty just in proportion as they do not waver and as they remain true to themselves.

In the midst of this constant wavering policy they will increase the conscious strength of the laboring masses just in proportion as their theory makes possible a logical, definite practice. The more the Socialist party maintains an indestructible power in the midst of the destruction of all authority, the more the Socialists will increase their authority. And the more they persevere in their irreconcilable opposition to the corruption of the ruling class the more complete the trust that will be vested in them by the great masses of the population in the midst of the universal rottenness which has today seized the bourgeois democracy, which has completely surrendered its principles for the purpose of gaining governmental favors.

The more immovable, logical and irreconcilable the Socialists remain, the sooner will they conquer their opponents.

It is to ask the Socialists to commit political suicide to demand that they join in any coalition or "bloc" policy, in any case where the words "reactionary mass" are truly applicable. It is demanding moral suicide of the Socialists to ask them to enter into an alliance with capitalist parties at a time when these have prostituted themselves and compromised themselves to the very bottom. Any such alliance would only be to join in furthering that prostitution.

Anxious friends fear that the Socialists may prematurely gain control of the government THROUGH a revolution. But if there is ever to be such a thing as a premature attainment of governmental power, it will come from the gaining of the appearance of governmental power BEFORE the revolution; that is, before the proletariat has actually gained political power. So long as it has not gained this, the Socialists can obtain a share in governmental power only by SELLING its political strength. The PROLETARIAT as a class can gain nothing in this man-

ner. Even in the best cases the only gain will be to the
PARLIAMENTARIANS who have carried out the sale.

Whoever looks upon the Socialist party as a means for
the freeing of the proletariat, must decisively oppose any
and all forms of participation by that party in the ruling
corruption. If there is anything that will rob us of the
confidence of all honorable elements in the masses, and
that will gain us the contempt of all those sections of the
proletariat that are capable of and willing to fight, and
that will bar the road to our progress, it is participation
of the Socialists in any coalition or "bloc" policy. .

The only elements that would be served by such a policy would be those to whom our party is nothing more
than a ladder by which they can personally climb—the
strivers and the self-seekers. The less of such elements
we attract to us and the more we can drive away, the
better for our battle.

How what has been said will be applied in individual
cases it is impossible to say definitely. Never was it more
difficult than now to foretell the form and tempo of the
coming developments, where all the factors that are to be
considered, with the exception of the proletariat, are so
indefinite, incalculable.

The only certain thing is universal uncertainty. It is
certain that we are entering upon a period of universal
unrest, of shifting of power, and that whatever form this
may take, or how long it may continue, a condition of
permanent stability will not be reached until the proletariat shall have gained the power to expropriate politically and economically the capitalist class and thereby
to inaugurate a new era in the world's history.

Whether this revolutionary period will continue as long
as that of the bourgeoisie, which began in 1789 and lasted
until 1871, is, naturally, impossible to foresee. To be sure,
all forms of evolution proceed much more rapidly now
than previously, but, on the other hand, the field of bat-

tle has grown enormously.   When Marx and Engels wrote the "Communist Manifesto" they saw before them only Western Europe as the battle field of the proletarian revolution.   Today it has become the whole world.   Today the battles in the struggle of the laboring and exploited class for freedom will be fought not alone upon the banks of the Spree and the Seine, but on the Hudson and the Mississippi, on the Neva and the Dardanelles, on the Ganges and the Hoangho.

Equally gigantic with the battle field are the problems that spring from it—the social organization of the world industry.

But the proletariat will arise from this revolutionary era, that may perhaps continue for a generation, wholly different from what it was when it went in.

If today the elite of the workers are the strongest, most far-seeing, unselfish, keenest, best and freest organized section of the nations of European civilization, then it will draw to itself in the fight and through the fight the most unselfish and far-seeing elements of all classes, and will organize and educate the backward elements within its own bosom and inspire them with the joy and hope of freedom.   It will raise its elite to the height of civilization and make them capable of directing that tremendous economic transformation that shall forever make an end of the whole world round of all misery arising from slavery, exploitation and ignorance.

Happy he who is called to share in this sublime battle and this glorious victory.